William Cotton

An Elizabethan Guild of the City of Exeter

An Account of the proceeding of the Society of Merchant Adventurers

William Cotton

An Elizabethan Guild of the City of Exeter
An Account of the proceeding of the Society of Merchant Adventurers

ISBN/EAN: 9783337178437

Printed in Europe, USA, Canada, Australia, Japan

Cover: Foto ©ninafisch / pixelio.de

More available books at **www.hansebooks.com**

EXETER QVAY,
IN THE 16TH CENTVRY.

AN ELIZABETHAN GUILD

OF THE

CITY OF EXETER.

AN ACCOUNT OF THE PROCEEDINGS OF

THE SOCIETY OF MERCHANT ADVENTURERS,

DURING THE LATTER HALF OF THE 16TH CENTURY,

BY

WILLIAM COTTON, F.S.A.,
MEMBER OF THE ROYAL ARCHÆOLOGICAL INSTITUTE OF GREAT BRITAIN AND IRELAND.

EXETER:
PRINTED FOR THE AUTHOR BY WILLIAM POLLARD, NORTH STREET.
1873.

TO THE

RIGHT WORSHIPFUL THE MAYOR OF EXETER,

CHARLES JOHN FOLLETT, ESQUIRE, B.C.L.,

THIS WORK

IS, BY PERMISSION, DEDICATED.

MDCCCLXXIII.

PREFACE.

The published histories of Exeter contain but one short paragraph relating to the most important of the Old City Guilds: it runs thus:—"1556 the Merchant Adventurers of this City trading to France and beyond the seas were incorporated by the Queen's Charter." The Queen here referred to is, of course, Mary, but it is doubtful if this Charter conveyed any substantial privilege or had any effect in stimulating commercial adventure.

The real foundation of the Guild dates undoubtedly from the original Charter granted by Queen Elizabeth, in which there is no reference whatever to a previous Charter. Certain services rendered to the Royal cause, in troublous times, is the only consideration expressed in the deed, for the privileges granted.

The absence of any allusion to this Guild by local historians is easily accounted for. John Hoker, the historian of the time, was a member of the Society, and was bound by his oath not to reveal its affairs, and when Isacke, his successor, wrote, the Society had been dissolved and left no trace, beyond a few scattered references to be found amongst the Municipal Archives. It is not until our own day that the proceedings of these Merchant Adventurers have been disclosed, and perhaps a better time could not have been selected than the present, with its gigantic commerce and daring speculation, to look back upon the time when the English trader first ventured to freight his own ships, and, under State encouragement, developed into the Merchant.

By the courtesy of the Master and Wardens of the Ancient Society of Weavers, Fullers and Shearmen, I have had placed at my disposal the minutes of the proceedings of the "Society of Merchant Adventurers trading beyond the Seas." These minutes are a record of transactions extending from the foundation of the Society to the end of the reign of Elizabeth; the papers were discovered amongst the archives of the Weavers' Society.

The commercial history of this period, generally speaking, yet remains to be written, and the interesting time when good Queen Bess was on the throne is treated of, by local historians, in a very scanty and summary manner. I have therefore thought it well to transcribe from these records, 'verbatim et literatim,' what appeared to me worthy of preservation, and the result is now presented to the reader with a commentary, (originally in the form of a Lecture delivered to the Members of the Exeter Literary Society) the shortcomings and defects in which will, I trust, be excused and lost sight of in the interest which should surround these episodes of a byegone age.

It will be seen that three hundred years ago Exeter occupied no mean position in the commercial world, and that her Merchants were men of mark. Their enterprize and intelligence is conspicuous, and not the least in the great work, for those days of the Canal, which, commenced in 1563, eventually opened a way for the shipping from the sea to Exeter Quay.

Apart from the convenience and saving of expense effected by thus being able to bring goods by water up to the walls of the City, there was the advantage of a snug and safe refuge, far from the estuary and under cover of the guns of the battery ; no mean consideration when the free rover would cut out a ship from Dartmouth Harbour, and carry off his prize.

The term "Adventurer" applied perhaps more to the prospect of the perils of the sea, and the contingency of loss by rovers and pirates, than to hazardous speculation in merchandize. We may fairly conclude that the judgment and caution of our Merchants prevented their being carried away with the adventurous enthusiasm of the times, and that their desire was to establish the "trade of merchandize" on a solid foundation. This is apparent in the anxiety to render those, who would at some time claim the right of admission to the Guild, worthy of membership. A long term of servitude was considered necessary for the apprentice, ere he could be trusted to set up for himself, and his interests and proper instruction had careful attention ; indeed it was not an unusual thing to send an apprentice to France, for a time, in order to acquire the language ; and this at the expense of the master to whom he was bound.

Apart from the commercial phase, we have revealed to us, in these minutes, glimpses of the social life of the period, and there is frequent reference to names which are still associated with the City : Above all, we make some acquaintance with such historic characters as Raleigh, Drake, Davis, and the Gilberts.

The Guild, probably, attained its greatest eminence in the next reign, and collapsed during the Parliamentary Wars. On the stone tablet in Bartholomew Yard, recording the consecration of the burial-ground in 1637, the Arms of the Merchant Adventurers and of Bishop Hall, who performed the ceremony, are placed one on either side of the Arms of the City.

PREFACE.

Three hundred years after his death is somewhat late in the day to pay a tribute to the memory of the Clerk to the Guild John Ffelde; but I cannot help expressing admiration at the exquisite care with which the first half of this Minute Book was kept. The specimens of caligraphy are simply perfect, and render the work of transcription comparatively an easy task.

With respect to the Illustrations, I have endeavoured, as far as possible, to give examples of the houses, which, it may reasonably be assumed, existed at the time. Nos. 78 and 79 Fore Street, Nos. 19 and 20 North Street, No. 46 High Street, and the corner of North Street with the figure of St. Peter, are still remaining, in good preservation; the engravings are from original drawings by Mr. Geo. Townsend, as are also the old houses in Frog Street, Westgate Street, and Red Lion Court, (since demolished), and the chimney-piece in Mallock's house. The representations of the Butchers' Row and the ancient Gates are from existing works. Northgate was removed in 1769, Eastgate in 1784, Westgate in 1815, Southgate in 1819, Watergate in 1615, and Broadgate in 1823. The last resident in the latter was the scavenger of the Close.

The Portraits were prepared expressly for this work. The first process—photographing from the faded oil-paintings—was one of considerable difficulty, but it was successfully accomplished, and the lithographs therefrom present a close resemblance to the originals. I am indebted to the courtesy of the Mayor (to whom this volume is dedicated) for permission to reproduce all of these with the exception of Hugh Crossing, and for that to the kindness of the Rev. H. Newport, Head Master of the Grammar School.

PREFACE.

The representation of Exeter Quay in the 16th century is not entirely an ideal picture. The old maps in the City Muniment Room enable us to draw the general features with accuracy, and the details are easily filled in from descriptive and other sources. With a desire to be strictly accurate I must express a doubt if there was an archway, like that depicted, in the Battery Tower; notwithstanding, I have allowed the statement to remain in the text until too late for revision. In the earliest known map of the City no opening is apparent, but in Speed's later map there are indications either of traffic through the tower to the mill-leat, or, what is more probable, they represent the waste water running from the Conduit which is wanting in the old map. It is not unlikely that the name "Battery-steps" is derived from some passage leading from the higher to the lower level, through the tower.

I am indebted to Moore's *History of Devonshire* for much information of a biographical character; and have to express my acknowledgments to many kind friends for their aid and encouragement.

STATUE OF HENRY VII. *See* Page 52.

INDEX TO NAMES.

Amye, E., 66, 67
Atwill, Lawrence, 36
Archer, Jno., 149
Aplyn, Mrs., 152
Aplyn, Jno., 49, 82
Alford, S., 55

Babb, Geffery, 64
Ball, Nichs., 64, 67
Barstable, Jno., 64
Bath, Earl of, 44, 45
Bath, Countess, 45
Bedford, Duke of, 45
Bedford, Earl of, 44, 50, 60, 118, 119
Bedforde, Countess, 45
Bevis, R., 43, 75, 160
Bickersteth, A., 131
Blackalle, 38, 55, 55, 141, 162, 163
Blackaller, J., 42, 67, 159
Blackaller, 66
Bodley, Canon, 94
Bodly, Sir T., 38
Bodlie, Jno., 23
Borough, Walter, 35, 141, 150
Bowchier, Lady F., 45
Boyer, Jas., 133
Bridgeman, T., 75
Brodcridge, C., 83
Browne, Thos., 31
Bruarton, T., 42, 49, 156, 159
Buckenham, W., 27, 37, 173
Buggins, W., 149
Buggins, Jno., 119
Buller, 38
Buller, Jno., 25

Calley, Harey, 161
Carey, Bishop, 52
Carwythen, Rd., 32
Chaffe, 38, 42, 93, 159, 165
Chapell, 64, 150
Chapell, T., 49, 75, 119, 150
Chapell, Wm., 42, 49, 159
Chappell, Jno., 43, 49, 75, 163
Cockerham, P., 66
Collishett, R., 125
Cotton, 169
Cotton, Robt., 26
Crossing, Hugh, 37, 79, 146, 155, 166,
Croston, Jno., 40

Dare, 64, 146
Davis, John, 80, 81
Davye, John, 40, 43, 44, 49, 50, 55, 119
Dennys, Sir R., 80, 149
Denys, Lady, 45
Dorchester, R., 43, 49, 55, 75, 84, 143, 146, 166, 167
Drake, Sir F., 87
Drake, Sir B., 90, 154
Ducke, W., 67
Ducke, Rd., 83

Edwardes, Tho., 55
Ellacott, 38, 42, 43, 55, 75, 126, 152, 160
Eron, 173
Essex, Lord, 45, 61, 128
Everie, 130,
Everyie, H., 67

Ffelde, Jno., 125
Fisher, T., 66
Fitzwarren Lord, 45
Follett, 38, 75

Gandie, Henry, 151
Geare, 38, 68, 175
Germyne, M., 42, 54, 141, 162, 166
Gilbert, Adrian, 81
Gilbert, Sir H., 85
Glanfeilde, 131
Grenewood, W., 148
Greynfelde, Sir R., 45
Gudridge, N., 73

Hackwill, Geo., 58
Hackewill, Jno., 26, 38, 49, 54, 75, 84, 143, 155,
Hackwill, Richd., 160
Hackwill, Wm., 38
Hawkes, J., 137
Hayman, N., 67
Hele, Jno., 37
Henley, R., 66
Hoker, Jno., 25, 35, 37, 47
Horsey, Jasper, 55, 148
Howell, Jno., 43
Hull, Henry, 43, 161
Hurste, Wm., 25, 31, 36, 42
Hutchyns, 42, 49, 50

Jopson, 77
Jurden, A., 154
Jurden, J., 38, 56

Knight, Simon, 31, 37, 42, 49

INDEX OF NAMES.

King James, 38, 39

Lake, P., 158
Lambell, R., 170
Lant, Jno., 36
Leach, Canon, 94, 169
Leach, Symon, 151
Leighton, Sir T., 67
Levermore, Morris, 26, 42
Levermore, P., 42, 49, 50, 67, 75
Locke, Edwd., 120

Mainwaring, 79, 85, 86, 146
Mallott, Jno., 56
Martin, Jno., 40, 117
Martin, Nich., 38, 39, 42, 43, 49, 50, 54, 55, 75, 141, 150, 160, 162, 163
Martin, Richd., 39
Martyn, Thos., 31, 37, 38, 39, 40, 42, 49, 50, 75, 158
Martin, Wm., 37, 38, 39, 42, 43, 49, 50, 54, 56, 58, 84, 147, 148, 150, 155, 158, 163, 166
Mauncell, Sir R., 168
Mayor of Plymouth, 94, 168
Medlande, 76
Mown, Sir W., 45
Mydwynter, Jno., 42
Mydwynter, Robt., 42

Newman, N., 67
Newman, R., 92, 158
Newlande of Totnes, 136
Newcombe, 94, 148
Newcombe, Wm., 169
Napers, I., 51

Owleborrowe, C., 124
Olyver, Eustace, 26, 31, 42, 158

Paramore, W., 64

Parker, Wm., 158
Parsons, Wm., 170
Peckham, Sir G., 85, 86
Peryman, 38, 42
Perrye, R., 141
Periam, Sir Wm., 35, 61, 128,
Periam, Jno., 23, 26, 35, 43, 49, 149
Periam, Geo., 49
Peter, Jno., 25, 26, 42.
Petter, Robt., 161, 162
Poulet, Sir A., 67,
Pope, Thos., 55, 67, 68
Pope, Jno., 42, 158
Portugal, King of, 40
Prestwood, Thos., 23, 26, 128, 167
Prowse, Richd., 159
Prouse, Jno., 37, 55, 61,
Prouse, W. 61, 128
37, 42, 55
Pyll Jno., 26

Raleigh, Sir. W., 80, 148
Richardson, T., 42
Russell, Lord, 23

Samwayes, H., 66, 67
Sampforde, Jno., 47, 49, 50, 120, 146, 150, 155, 166, 167
Saunderson, Wm., 83, 149
Sandye, Wm., 146, 166
Saunders, Mr., 45
Saunders, S., 83
Saverye, C., 67, 130
Seldon, L., 129
Selwood, Phillibert, 66, 67
Shapley, R., 137
Shere, Jno., 64
Sherwoode, R., 76
Skynner, J., 66
Smith, Gilbert, 141
Smith, Geo., 37, 55, 43, 149, 162

Snape, Revd. E., 91, 92, 157
Snowe, Thos., 168
Sonds, Capt., 94, 168
Southcott, T., 83
Spicer, T., 37, 43, 49, 76, 155, 160, 162
Spicer, Nicholas, 37, 43, 49, 50, 51, 75, 81
Spicer, C., 37, 43, 54
Spicer, W., 37, 43, 54, 166, 167
Spurway, 38
Stafforde, Sir E.
Stubbes, W., 49, 50, 51
Swete, Rd., 64, 158
Swete, R., 49, 76, 119
Swete, Mrs., 152

Tailor, Jno., 54, 155
Toker, F., 119
Toker, N., 119, 171
Toker, Jno., 28, 29
Trowyth, Wm., 26
Trewe, Jno., 48, 50
Trigge, Pawle, 143
Tryvett, L., 67
Tryvett, W., 42, 49
Tucker, Wm., 163, 164
Tuckfield, Joan, 37, 55
Turner, Capt., 167

Vylvayne, Davye, 119
Vynton, Robt., 31

Walker, T., 37, 43, 160, 166
Walsingham, Sir T., 85, 149
Watkins, John, 163
Weekes, Jno., 140
Welch, Wm., 154
Wilforde, 143, 144
Wyot, P., 45
Wyse, Jno., 64

Yarde, 38, 42, 49, 50, 64
Yonge, Jno., 83

GENERAL INDEX.

Abbots of Buckfastleigh, 45
Accounts, 176
Act against stubborness, &c., 28
Action at Guildhall, 163
Algarbe, 31
Alman Ryvets, 120
Almshouses, 36, 41
Alneger's Fees, 79, 148
America, Gilbert's expedition to, 85
Apprentices, 60, 92, 158, 169, 172
Arbitrators, 158
Arms of the Guild, 11
Armada, Spanish, 78
Arrow Slits, 53
Auditors, 55
Average Money, 28, 57, 109
Award, 170
Axminster, 83

Balance Sheet, 95
Bampfylde House, 45
Bar of Exmouth, 151
Barnstaple, Town Clerk of, 45
Bastions, 52
Battery Steps, 53
Bear Inn, 47
Bedford Circus, 44
Bedford House, 44, 118
Behaviour of Citizens, 26
Bell Hill, 47
Bellman by night, 61
Bishop's Palace, 52
Black Assize, 89, 154

Black booke, 56
Bondsmen pay, 57
Brawling and Fighting, 123
Broker, 93, 161
Buck, 120
Buckets, 133
Burial of Spaniard, 77, 143

Calverley, 83
Calyver, 44, 119, 120
Canal, 48
Canon Leach intercedes, 94
Carrying trade, 29
Catherine St., 44
Chamber vote sugar loaves, 94
China, trade with, 83
Chapel Chamber, 32
Chapel Chamber of Guildhall, 25
Charter granted, 23, 24, 25
Charter, 1
Chard, 66, 67, 83, 142, 161
Charities, 35, 37
Christopher of Dartmouth, 32
Civic Guard, 44
Clerk, 125, 136
Clerk appointed, 60
Cloth Merchants, 32
Cockctes, 148
College Kitchen, 47
College, Exeter, 38
College, Pembroke, 39
Commission to fit out ships 76, 138, 139
Company Establishe l, 25,

Committees to assess damages, 143
Contentions, 59
Conveyance, 51
Coombe, St., 46
Corsletts, 44, 120
Corn, 88, 89, 150 to 153
Countess Wear, 48
Councellor, 147
Cranage, 49, 50, 51
Crediton, 35
Creedy Park, 40
Crokes, 133
Cullompton, 83, 148
Customs abuses, 79, 145
Customs duties, 79, 145

Dartmouth, 32, 82, 83, 142
Davis's adventure, 82, 83, 84
Davye's Almshouses, 41
Davye's House, 41
Davye's Garden, &c., 41
Dean and Chapter, 165
Decorative fittings, 46
Defence against Raleigh, 148, 149
Difficulties with Brittany, 136, 137
Difficulties with Spain, 77, 142
Dinner, 57, 58, 121, 122
Discipline, 27
Disturbed state of Channel, 93, 94, 166, 168
Douceur, 77, 94, 168
Drake's letter, 87
Drum bought, 61
Dunkirks, 94, 166, 167

GENERAL INDEX.

Easterlings, 30
Election day, 54
Embrasures, 53
Examples of Minutes, 167
Excessive Duties, 97
Exclusive trading, 177
Excuse for taking oath, 165
Exeter Sound, 84
Exe, 48
Exmouth, 49
Expedition to China, 82

Famine, 58, 88, 89, 150
Felts, 124
FINES—
  Jno. Pyll, 26, 108
  H. Maunder's 27
  W. Buckenam's, 27
  Non-attendance, 27
  Slackness, 27
  Absence, 28, 57
  Absence of Governor, 29
  Absence of Consuls, 29
  Not wearing gowns, 56, 174
  Quarrelling, 59
  Foul words, 58, 59
  Assault, 59
  Smuggling, 162, 164, 173, 174
  Arbitrators, 158
  Leaving table, 174
  Adventuring, 174
  For admission, 174
First election day, 25
First venture as Shipowners, 31
Fish, 154
Fleming, 154
French Suit, 66
Fustian, 124

Gables, 46, 47
Gandy St., 46
Gaol Fever, 89, 90, 154
Garnett, 152
Gascon Wines, 79, 147
Gilbert Sound, 84
Goblet, 27
Goddes pony, 31
Goldsmith St., 46

Golden Hind, 89
Governor of Brittany, 133
Grammar School, 37
Grey Friars, 43
Guardships, 94
Guernsey, 134
Guildhall Portraits, 35, 36, 37
Guildhall rebuilt, 90 155
Guildhall, 32, 35 155, 163
Gunpowder, 77, 120, 140, 141, 142, 168

Hall Merchants, 32
Haven, 48
Havre de Grace, 29
Herring-bone work, 53

Fleming Shipowners, 30.
High St., 46
Hoker's Oration, 99
Holy Howst, 144
Honiton. 23
House Money, 175
Hurst's servant, 115

Imposition on Wine, 147
India trade, with, 83
Infringement of liberties, 93, 160
Injuries by Spain, 143, 144
Inns of Court, 39
Inner Temple, 39
Inquisition, 77
Inventory, 34
Italian Shipowners, 30

Jan's Cross, 46
Jersey, 133
Juberaltare, 32

Kersaics, 124, 130
Key of Topsham, 51
King's Arms Sluice, 48

Lack of Ships for Service of Mary, 30
Larkbeare House, 43
Lease of Hall, 33
Leads of Guildhall, 90
Letters Patent to Gilbert and others, 81
Letter to Totnes, 129

Letters of Mark, 94
Letter from Commissioners in London and Reply, 64, 65
Little Quay-lane, 47
London Guildhall, 142
Lord Mayor's Proclamation, 26
Lottery, 29, 109
Lyme, 72, 142, 161
Lyncoln's Inn, 131

Mallocs, 134
Mantlopiece, 46
Marriage of Lady E. Russell, 44, 119
Martin, Jno., special admission, 117
Mariners' Wyndage, 120
Martin, W., disbursments, 115
Mary Arches, 38, 40, 41, 46
Mayor, 35, 36, 37, 38, 39
Merchants' Hall, 32, 33
Merchants in Villages, 92, 130, 159
Members of Parliament, 37, 39
Members, accession of, 94
Mermaid, 83
Midsummer Eve, 44, 118
Miscellanea, 169
Monopoly, 26, 29
Monument Davy's, 40
Moonshine, 82, 83
Morlais, 134
Morlais, Barkes in, 133
Murder, 61
Music, 90, 91
Muster at Earl Bedford's 44, 118, 119

New Cut, 48
Night Caps, 61
North Star, 83
North West Passage, 81, 149

Oaths of the Officers, 19
Old room, 46
Oliver's History, 48
Oration by Hoker, 25, 99,

GENERAL INDEX.

Ostend, Siege of, 94

Pampoole, 162
Pancras Lane, 46
Petition of P. Cane, 89, 153
Pirates, 138, 140
Plague, 29, 38, 110
Policy of Elizabeth, 24, 30
Policy of Guild, 27
Poltimore, 46
Poole, 75
Port, 51
Port dues, conveyance of, 51
Preacher, 91, 156, 157
Preston St., 46
Protest, 97
Public Preacher, 91, 156, 157

Quadrangle, 46, 47
Quatre Voix, 47,
Queen's Ships, 76, 138, 139, 140
Queen's Watch, 44, 118

Raden Lane, 45
Raleigh's proposal, 149
Recorder, 39
Refusal to take oath, 93, 165
Refusal to be Governor, 35, 114
Relief for poor, 88, 152
Rent of Hall, 33
Reprisals, 77
Restitution by Spain, 142
Review, 44, 118
Rougemont Castle, 52
Rovers, 94
Russell, Lady E., 44, 110
Rye, 88, 89, 150, 151, 152

St. David's, 43
St. George's Bell, 32
St. George's Church, 47
St. George's Chapel, 32
St. Leonard's Wear, 48
St. Sidwell's, 43, 47
Sandridge, 81
Seal, 175
Sergeant at Mace, 154
Sergeant, 56
Sherys, 32
Shipping, 31, 47, 108, 111
Siege of Exeter, 23
Sumptuary Laws, 92, 159
Smuggling, 93, 124, 162, 163
Snayle Tower, 53
Southernhay, 43, 44
South St., 47
Spaniards, 78
Southgate, 43, 47
Spanish Company, 33, 78, 80, 144, 145
Special fellowship, 117
Squirrell, 87
Stagnation of trade, 29
Standing Counsel, 39
Star Chamber, 164
Statutes and ordinances, 14
Strosse, 28
Stubborne, 28
Subscription for Corn, 89, 152
Suit to France, 66
Sunshine, 82, 83

Tailors, quarrel with, 25
Taunton, 66, 67, 83, 142, 160
Tawstock Court, 45
Tiverton, 66, 67, 83, 142, 161

Topsham, 48, 49, 50, 143
Totnes, 66, 67, 83, 129, 142, 160
Totnes, Merchants' letter from, 62, 63
Trade with France, 62
Treasurer's Balance Sheet, 95
Trenchard's Sluice, 48
Trewe, Jno., 48
Trew's Wear, 48
Tucker's Hall, 46
Turf, 48,

Unpaid debts, 175

Valiant Soldier, 43
Vintners' Licenses, 80
Vitterio Canvas, 124
Waits, 90, 91
Walk under Guildhall, 155
Wall, City, 52, 53
Watch, Midsummer, 44, 118
Watercourse, 51
Watergate, 47, 53 120
Wharffage, 49
Whitware, 162
Whysselers, 119
Widows, 152
Will of Ellacott, 126
Winchester, Lord, 30
Woodhouse, 47, 120
Wood for Poor, 120
Woollen Clothes, duties on, 146,
Wyndage, 120
Wynard's Hospital, 44
Wyott's Diary, 88
Yarn Market, 47

INDEX TO ILLUSTRATIONS.

Exeter Quay	Frontispiece.
St. Peter, corner of North Street	Page ix.
Arms of the Guild	,, 13
Hoker, John	,, 22
The Guildhall	,, 22
Periam, John	,, 26
Houses in Frog Street, West Quarter	,, 28
Old Houses at West Gate	,, 32
Borough, Walter	,, 34
Hurst, William	,, 36
Crossing, Hugh	,, 38
Atwill, Lawrence	,, 40
Old Butcher Row	,, 42
No. 46, High Street	,, 44
Chimney Piece in Mallock's House Gandy Street	,, 46
Corner of North Street	,, 47
The Watergate (Exterior)	,, 48
The South Gate (Exterior)	,, 50
The West Gate (Exterior)	,, 50
Entrance Gateway to the Castle	,, 52
Statue of Henry VII., No. 266, High Street	,, 52
No. 78 & 79, Fore Street	,, 54
Red Lion Court, Magdalen Street	,, 58
The North Gate (Exterior)	,, 60
The East Gate (Exterior)	,, 64
No. 19 & 20, North Street	,, 88
Staircase in "King John Tavern," formerly in South Street	,, 76
The Broadgate (Interior)	,, 92
Map of Exeter, at the end of the Book.	

SUBSCRIBERS.

	Copy.
Albrecht, C. S., Exeter	1
Andrews, Biggs, Q.C., Heavitree	1
Barnes, Rev. Preb., R. H., Heavitree	2
Bastard, B. J. P., Kitley, Plympton	1
Battishill, W. J., Exeter	1
Bayley, W. Rutter, Cotford, Sidmouth	1
Bedford, His Grace the Duke of, 82, Eaton Square, London	4
Birkmyer, J. B., Exeter	1
Bocket, the Rev. J., Exeter	1
Boger, Deeble, Wolsdon Antony, Devonport	1
Bodley, A., Exeter	1
Bremridge, T. J., Exeter	1
Buckingham, Wm., Exeter	1
Cann, Wm., Exeter	1
Chanter, J. R., Barnstaple	1
Chichester, Robt., Hall, Barnstaple	1
Clarke, Henry, Exeter	1
Cole Cole, W., Exmouth	1
Coleridge, Sir J. Duke, Q.C., M.P.	1
Cooper, George, Exeter	1
Cotton, J. K., Barnstaple	2
Cotton, R. W., Barnstaple	1
Cotton, F. J., 7, Bedford Row, London	1
Dacie, G. L., Exeter	1
Davy, Fras., Topsham	1
Dangar, Rev. J. G., Exeter Diocesan Training College	1
Devon, Rt. Honble. the Earl of, Powderham Castle	1
Drayton and Sons, Messrs., Exeter	2
Durant, R., Sharpham	1
D'Urban, W. S. M., Albuera, Mount Radford	1
Doidge, J. G., Lifton, Launceston	1
Dymond, Robert, F.S.A., Exeter	1

SUBSCRIBERS.

Ellis, Henry S., Exeter	1
Ellis, W. Horton, Exeter	1
Eland, H., Exeter	6
Floud, T., Exeter	1
Foweraker, Rev. E. T., Exeter	1
Galton, Rev. J. L., Exeter	1
Geare, John, Exeter	3
Gill, H. S., Tiverton	1
Gray, T. W., Heavitree	
Hamilton, A. H. A., Fairfield Lodge, Exeter	1
Harding, Lieut.-Col., Barnstaple	1
Harding, Joseph, Exeter	1
Hayward, P. B., Exeter	1
Head, R. T., The Briars, Alphington	1
Head, R. W., Exeter	1
Hedgeland, Rev. Prebendary, Penzance	1
Hippisley, J. H., Shobrooke	10
Hooper, H. W., Exeter	3
Huyshe, the Rev. John, Clisthydon	1
Jackson, J., Southernhay, Exeter	1
James, H. M., Exeter	1
Kendall, William	1
Kingdon, Kent, Exeter	1
Kingdon, G. C., Exeter	1
Laidman, C. J., Newcastle-on-Tyne	1
Lewis, Charles, Exeter	1
Lloyd, Horace C., Exeter	1
Luke, A. F., Exeter	1
Luxmoore, W., Jun., Exeter	1
Matthews, Henry, Bradninch	2
Miles, W., Exeter	1
Milford, Frederick, Exeter	1
Milne, A. D., Exeter	1
Moore, W. D., Town Clerk, Exeter	1
Mortimer, W., Exeter	1

SUBSCRIBERS.

Pennell, Dr., Venbridge, Cheriton Bishop	1
Periam, John, Bampton	1
Pollard, F., Exeter	1
Richards, W. J., Exeter	1
Snow, T. M., Exeter	2
Snow, William, Exeter	1
Snow, E. N., Exeter	1
Shapter, Dr., Exeter	1
Smith, W. T., Baring Crescent, Heavitree	1
St. Aubyn, W. J., Sheffield Barracks	1
Strother, Rev. J. B., Alphington	1
Teesdale, C. L. M., 18, Randolph Crescent, Maida Vale, London	1
Thomas, J. L., Newhayes, St. Thomas	1
Thomas, H. D., Exeter	1
Townsend, George, Exeter	1
Tucker, Chas., Marlands	1
Turner, C. H., Dawlish	1
Varwell, Peter, St. Thomas	1
Vicary, Wm., Exeter	1
Wainwright, T., Literary Institution, Barnstaple	1
Wilcocks, Henry, Spurbarn, Mount Radford	1
Woods, Major, Devon and Exeter Club	1

ERRATA.

Page 42 line 2 for "*John* Hurst," read "*William* Hurst."
,, 61 ,, 3 for "*John* Ellacott," read "*Henry* Ellacott."
,, 76 ,, 9 for "*the* nations," read "*other* nations."
,, 83 ,, 6 for "*Duche*," read "*Ducke*."

The Charter granted to the Merchant Adventurers of the City of Exeter by Queen Elizabeth.

ELIZABETH by the grace of God Queene of Englande, ffrance, and Irlande, defender of the faith, etc. To all to whome this present wrytinge shall come greetinge, Knowe ye that wee, in consideracion of the good trewe and faithfull obedyence and servise, done by the maio' and citizens of our Citie of Excester, aswell in the tyme of o^r moste welbeloved grandfather Kinge Henry the Seventh : as nowe of late, in the tyme of oure welbeloved brother Kinge Edwarde the Syxt, ageinst dyverse treasones and rebellions being moved and sturred in that dayes. And also for the speciall favoure and love which wee have and doo beere to oure welbeloved and faithfull subjectes, nowe citizens of oure saide Citie of Excester : Desiring the good contynuance and happie succession and increase of the same. And also for taking awaie, abolisshinge, and amovinge, of many and sundrie obsurdities and inconveniences which of late within the saide Citie hath cropen in and growen by reason of the excessive nomber of artificers and other inexpert ignorante and unworthie men which doo take upon them to use the arte scyence and mysterie of merchandise : and trafique of merchant wares to the greate detriment of the commonwealth of this oure realme of Englande. And also for dyverse other good consideracions especiallie moving us thereunto. Of oure especiall grace, and of oure certain knowledge and meere mocion : wee will graunte and ordeyne for us oure heires and successors ; and by thes presentes we geve especiall lycence, unto our

B

welbeloved Robert Mydwynter, John Buller, William Hurste, John Blackall the elder, John Mydwynter, William Bucknam, Morrys Levermore, Walter Staplehill, John Peter thelder, John Wolcote, John Blackall, Richard Prestwood, Harry Maunder, Peter Lake, Thomas Lambert, Thomas Richardson, Thomas Prestwood, Symon Knyght, Eustace Olyver, William Chapell, Gilbert Saywell, Nicholas Martyn, John Vowels als Hoker, William Tryvet, Mychael Germyn, Edmonde Whetcombe, Thomas Marshall, Edwarde Lymet, William Waye, John Barstable, Hubert Colwyll, Phillipp Yarde, Richard Zelwod, Richard Haselwodd, William Seldon, Thomas Spycer, Andrewe Gere, Robert Hunte, John Lawgher, Richard Mawdyt, Richarde Hockley, Harry Ellacote, Richarde Gybbe, Harry Robertes, William Hunte, John Hyll, John Budley, John Hychens, and John Hewet: Nowe beinge marchauntes adventurers of o^r saide Citie of Excester, and unto their successors marchauntes adventurers of o^r saide Citie for ever, and to others which are or shalbe of their Societie, one Governor and fower Consuls, which may the better governe and rule the state of all things belonging to the said marchantes. The which Governo' Consulls and whole Societie of Marchantes Adventurers of the saide Citie by the name of a Governo' Consulls and Societie of Marchantes Adventurers of the Citie of Excester, trafiquing the realme of ffraunce and dominions of the ffrenche kinge: That they be and shalbe one bodye corporate and politique and one whole companye in deede, worde, and name, and them and their successors wee ordeyne, establyshe, create, erect, incorporate, and unite together, by the same name, one bodye corporate and politique in deede, worde, and name, by thes presentes for ever to endure, and to have perpetuall succession. And further that oure entencion may take moore worthie effect towardes the benefyt of the saide marchantes, wee will and by thes presentes graunte that the forenamed and our welbeloved John Peter thelder, be and shalbe the fyrst newe Governo', and the foresaid and oure welbeloved William Hurste, John Mydwynter, Gilbert Saywell, and Symon Knyght, be and shall be the firste newe Consulls of the companye of the foresaid marchants. And furthermore we will, and by thes presentes graunte for us, o^r heires, and successors, to the saide Governo' Consulls and Societie, and to their successors for ever. That they and their successors, by the foresaide name of a Governo' Consuls and Societie of Merchants Adventurers of the Citie of Exon traffiquinge the realme of Ffraunce and dominions of the Ffrenche Kinges, be hable and expert in the lawe, to searche out, to perceave, to receave, to have and to holde to theim and to their successors in ffee and perpetuitie, or by any other waies, to the better supportinge of the burdens of the forsaide marchantes daylie growing and happening; as well of oure heires or successors, as of any other parson or parsons whatsoever (all kynde of goodes, cattalles, lordshippes, manors, mesuages, landes, tenements, advowsions, and other proffyetes and hereditaments), that will sell, geve, graunte, yealde, alienate, enfeoffe, or confirme the same, so that it do not excede, in the whole, above the yerely valewe of one hundred marks besides all charges and reprises, by the lycence of the highe lordes of the same. The statute of settynge of landes and tenementes to mortmayne or any other Statute Act, ordynance, proviso, proclamacion, or restraynt to the contrary before this tyme set forth, ordeyned, or provided, in any wise notwithstandinge.

AND that the saide Goevrnor, Consulls, and Societie, by the saide name, may sue and be sued, defende and be defended answer and be answered, in all and singler actions, quarrells, sutes, and demandes whatsoever, as well reall and parsonall and myxt, or of what kynde or nature so ever they be, and before whatsoever oᵣ Justice or Judge, or before every oure Justices or Judges, or any other oure Officers or Mynisters of us, oᵣ heires and successors, or any other whatsoever within this oure Realme of Englande, or Marcheses of the same: or in whatsoever Courte and other place, and in whatsoever Courtes and other places of us ovre heires and successors, or of any other within oure Realme of Englande or Marcheses of the same. And that they have one common seale to serve in their busyns for ever in tyme to come.

AND farther we will and by thes presentes, for us, our heires, and successors, Doo geve and grannte lycence to the Governo', Consulls, and Societie, and to their saide successors, that they or the greater parte of the same marchantes maye yerelie and successivelie chuse and mak in every the syxt daye of August, one Governo' and fower Consulls, which shall remayne in their saide offices the space of one whole yeare: The which Governo' and Consulls (a Corporall othe beinge first ministred) the common affaires of the saide societie may and shall support, and have care of and of the same societie and misterie. As also of all and singular parsons whatsoever of the saide Citie of Excester, usinge the mistercy of marchandise and merseres, and those that shall serve theim their servantes, apprentises, and factors, and also the marchandise, marchant, wares, merceries, and every kynde of the same to cause to be oversene, rewled, governed, and corrected, from tyme to tyme as it shall seeme to theim most expedient, accordinge to the lawes and statutes among theim made in this behalfe. And that they (as often tymes as to theim shall seeme expedient, for suche entent and purpose) may of theim selves, make lawfull and honest assembles in all suche kynde of places and haules, as by theim shalbe erected or appointed. And that among themselves, they may make, setfurth, and ordeyne, as many and singler reasonable and holsome statutes, lawes, and ordynaunces, for the good rewle and governaunce of all their goodes, cattalls, landes, tenementes, and hereditamentes, as of the Governo', Consulls, and Societie, and of all and singular parsons of the same societie, not only of occupiers but also of sarvauntes, and suche as doo serve in the same mystery; as also for the correction and ponyshement of the faulctes in the same whatsoever, as it shall seeme from tyme to tyme to theim best expedient. And also that the saide statutes, lawes, and ordynaunces, when and as often as they byst shall abolyshe, make voyde, frustrate, alter, and channge, and other newe statutes at their pleasure maye ordeyne, set, observe, and commaunde from tyme to tyme accordinge to their good discrecions as it shall best please theim. Soo that the saide statutes lawes and ordynaunces, or any parte or partes thereof be not repugnant or contrary to the customable lawes statutes and ordynaunces of oure Realme of England, or oure saide Citie of Excester, the which wee commande, and will to be observed inviolatelie.

AND also we have graunted to the Governo' and his saide Consulls and Companye, and to their saide successors, that when and as often as it doeth happen, any or one of theim, the saide Governo' and Consulls, after being chosen into any of the offices aforesaide to dye before the determinacion of one whole yeare next and imediatelie folowing the daye of suche election, or before the prefixt ende of his continuacion in the saide office, or wyllinglie doo goo awaye from his office by any cause or meanes whatsoever, soo that he is not able nor cannot observe, fulfill, and execute his office and place accordinglie, Or ells yf hee or they doo refuse or neclect to execute suche an office: That then the saide Governo^{rs}, Consulls, and Societie, or the greater parte of theim may lawfullie and freelie be hable, and shall chewse and appoynte some other honest man or men of the foresaide companye, in the place of hym or theim so dyeing, departinge, refusinge, or neclectinge, for the residue of the yeare folowinge and contynewing: and that from tyme to tyme as often as it shall soo happen. AND FARTHER of our ample grace, and for the consideracions aforesaide, as also for the greater quietnes and welth of the saide Merchantes wee will and by thes presentes doo ordeyne and establishe and also forbyd, that none of the citizens or inhabitance of oure saide cytie of Excester, nether of the Countie of the saide Citie, of what estate, degree, or condition soever hee bee, doo from hensforth presume or dare to transporte delyver, shipp, or convey any kynde of marchandies, marchantwares, or merceres to the saide Realme of ffraunce or any other the Kinge of ffraunce, his dominions out of this oure realme, nor to bringe in or convey, or cause to be brought in or conveyed, by any meanes, any kinde of marchant wares, merceres, or marchandise, from the saide realme of ffraunce, or the frenche kynges dominions into this our realme (the marchanntes aforesaide onlie excepted) upon payne of a grevous fyne,¹ or other kinde of punyshement upon theim reasonable to be set or done, except he be first free of the saide company accordinge to the determinacion in that behalf to be ordeyned.

AND farther, of oure more abundant grace, wee ordeyne, will, grauntе, and by thes presentes doo firmelie adioyne and commaunde That all and singler artificers of our said Citie, which will exercise, doo, and frequent the mysterie and arte of mer-

---

¹ [Oure great displeasure] *erased*.

ceries and marchandize, and doo request to be of the Companye of the saide Merchantes within three yeares next followinge be freelie admytted and receaved into the saide societie and freedome of the same marchantes, to use, have, and enioye the liberties and privileges unto theim graunted, without fine or some of money or any other kynde of thinge for the same to be paied and that in as ample maner and forme as here in thes o^r letters is speciallie noiated. So that after the receavinge or admyssion of any craftes man the same doo desiste and leave the exercise, occupacion and use of his handye crafte and mysterie.

AND in lyke manner we ordeyne, will, and commande, under the payne of a grevouse ffyne (for the greater benefit of the saide Marchauntes) that every parsone, by thes letters patente, incorporate or to be incorporated, and now erected or made a marchant and exersysinge, occupying, and frequentinge or using any arte or handyes mysterie doo dessiste and utterlie geave hymself from the exercyse and occupacion of suche his handye crafte, orells that hee utterlie leave the arte of merceries and marchandise and the exercise, use, and trafiquing of the same.

AND farther, consideringe that artificers and users of handye crafte and mysteries be necessarie members of a common welth, and wee desiringe therefore utterlie to take awaye and extinguishe many evells which in time to come may creepe in to the comon welth. Yf every artificer of the saide Citie of Exseter shoulde be suffered at his owne will and choyse and whensoever hee lyste to be receaved and admytted into the felowshipp and libertie of the saide Marchantes Adventurers ; wee ordeyne, will, . and commande, that after the terme of three years, next folowinge the date of this our letteres patentes no parson of what estate or condicion soever he be, be receved or admytted in to the societie and libertie of the saide Marchantes Adventurers except his admission and receaving be hadd and done by the common consent and assent of the Company of the saide Marchantes or the greater parte of theim to be done by payment of some reasonable fyne upon the saide parson to be levied by the same companye and their officers for the better supportinge of the charges and expences of the same Governo', Consulls, and Societie daylie growinge and happeninge, except any such myght demaunde to be admytted and receved in to the saide libertie and societie by reason of his patrimonye or of his service done after the maner of apprentise even as the custome and order is of marchantes adventurers which doo frequente the lowe countries and province of fflaunders. AND MOREOVER that the premisses and all statutes, lawes, ordynaunces and commaundementes of the saide Governo', Consulls, and Societie, may in tyme to come, be the better observed, done and obeyed: wee have graunted for us oure heires, and successors, unto the saide Governo' and Consulls, and to there successors full power and authoritie (by the teano^r of the presentes) to make serche and serches, among all the trafiquors and users of the mysterie, or arte of marchandize, and of all merceries, marchant wares, and marchandises, of wayghtes, measures, and other thinges incident or respecting the said mysterie: And to make inquisicion, vewe, and examinacion; and of takinge and haveinge, correcting, and reformynge of the defaulete in the same, and of ponysshinge and abolysshinge the defaulete by due and lawfull manes. And that 'pon the same offenders, ageinst the teano^r of thes o^r letters patentes or any other premisses, or ageynst the reasonable ordynaunce and honest lawes and statutes of the same Governo', Cons^{ll} of and Societie to be ordeyned, as in forme aforesaide: to put, appoynte, sett, execute, levye, and commaunde, fynes, amerciamentes, paynes, penalties, imprisonmentes by bodye or goodes accordinge to the order and discrecion of the Governo' and Consulls, with thadvise and assistance of the Maior of oure saide Citie of Excester and fower Aldermen of the same Citie for the time being, accordinge to the lawes of this our Realme of England: AND the same fynes, amerciamentes, paynes, penalties, imprisonmentes, and ponysshmentes, shalbe liable to remytt, release, moderate, chaunge, and alter, according to the discrecion and by thadvise of the saide assistance, when and as often as neade shall requier from hensforth and as it shall best seeme to the same Governo' and Consulls with th advise of the saide assistance. OF THE WHICH FINES amerciamentes, and payments of money to be set and put upon suche offenders and transgressors for their contemptes offences or defauletes as in forme aforesaide, wee will and graunte for us o heires and successors ffrom tyme to tyme, in every the feaste of Saint Mychaell tharchaungell thone moytie or halfendeale, to be levied and geven to the proper use and behofe of the Chamber of the Comynaltie of o^r saide Citie of Excester, in consideracion that the saide Maio^r and Aldermen of the same Citie doo assist and healpe the said Governo' and Consulls ffrom tyme to tyme in executing and doing the premisses. AND the other halfendeale or moytie of the same wee will and graunt by thes presentes to be levyed, converted, and given (as in forme aforesaid) to the onelye and proper use and healpe of the Societie of the saide Marchantes: to be hadd and holden unto theim of our gyfte, without accompte or anye other thinge to be rendered, paid, or done in that behalffe, to us, our heires or successors, anye statute, acte, ordynaunce, provisyon, or restrainte, hade, made, sett fourthe, ordeyned, or provided to the contrarye, or any other kind of thinge, cause, or matter whatsoever in any wise not withstandinge. IN

CONSIDERATION of all whiche and singuler premisses as aforesside by us graunted, establyshed and ordeyned the same Governo', Consulls, and Societie, have graunted and faithfullie promised for them and their said successors that they and their saide successors will yerely enlarge and distribute in tyme to come, unto twelve poore and impotent people of the saide Citie, twelve garments of clothe, that is to saye to everye of them one garment of clothe ; and that also from tyme to tyme (asmuch as in theim lyeth) will relyve and healpe all suche of their saide Companye, as by infortunacie and force of the sea, or by other meanes doo faule into povertie or necessitie. FFOR that expresse mencion of the certentie or trewe yerelie valewe, or any other valewe, of the premisses, or any of theim, or of other gyftes or grauntes, by us or by any of our progenitors or predecessors to the foresaide Governo', Consulls, and Societie, or to any of them or others. before this tyme made, or in thes presentes done, doeth litle appere. OR any other statute, acte, ordynaunce, provisione, proclamation, or restraynte to the contrarye in this behalfe, before this set furthe done, ordayned, or provided, or any other thinge, cause, or matter whatsoever in any wyse notwithstanding. IN WITNESS whereof wee have caused thes oure letters to be made patentes. MY self being witness given at Westminster the seventeenth day of June in the seconde yeare of oure reigne.

> Done by the Queen herself and of the date as
> aforesaid by authoritie of Parliament.

The Arms of the Guild.

The trewe copie of the graunte of the Armes geven unto this Societie by Clarencieulx, principal heralde and Kynge of Armes, etc., in the seconde yeare of the reigne of our Sovereigne Lady Queene Elizabeth, which is as foloweth:

TO ALL AND SINGULER as well kinges, herauldes, and officers of armes, as nobles, gentlemen, and others which thes presentes shall se or heare, WILLIAM HARVYE, Esquier, otherwise called Clarenciaulx principall heralde and Kinge of Armes of the Sowthe Easte and West partes of the Realme of Englande, Sendeth due comendacions and greetinge. Fforasmoche as auncientlie from the begynninge, the valiant and vertuous actes of excellent parsons hath byn commended to the worlde, with sundrie monumentes and rememberances of their good desertes amongest the which the chiefest and most usual hath byn the bearinge of signes and tokens in Shyldes called Armes, being no other thinges then evidences and demonstracions of prowes and valoure dyverslie distributed, accordinge to the qualites and desertes of the parsons: To thyntent that suche as have done commendable servise to their prince or contrey, ether in warre or peace, or by the laudable and couragiouse procedinges in the augmentacion of the estate or comen welth of their natyve-realme, or countrye, myght both receave due hono^r in their lyves: But also deryve the same successively to their posterities and successors after them. AND WHEREAS the Queenes moste royall majestie, consideringe the forwardnes and industrie of the right worshipfyll companye and felowshipp of the marchantes adventurers of her highnes Citie of Excester, who sekethe all the good meanes and waies possible for the mayn,

tenaunce of the estate and common welth of her Mat^ies
saide Citie of Excester, IN consideracion whereof and for
the further encoragement of the saide marchantes hath
erected, established, and made theim a Bodeye pollytyke,
And incorporated theim by the names of Governors Consulls
Assistauntes and Marchants Adventurers and their successors
in the saide corporacion for evermore by her highnes letters
patentes under the Great Seale of England wherefore the
premisses consydered. The saide Clarencieulx king of armes for
a further manyfestacions of the same and also that it maye
appere unto the worlde their laudable and coragious enterprises,
so that they have well meryted and deserved to have assigned
unto them tokens and ensignes of honour for the further increase
of their worshippes; whereupon the said Clarencieulx Kinge
of Armes by power and authoritie annexed attributed geven
and granted to me and to my office of Clarencieulx Kinge of
Armes By letters patentes under the greate seale of Englande
have devised, ordeyned, geven, and granted to the whole Bodye
of the saide Corporacion whereof at this present tyme is Governor
John Peter, Esquirr, William Hurst, John Mydwynter, Gilbert
Saywell, and Symon Knight, Consulls: Robert Mydwinter, John
Buller, John Blackaller, William Bucknam, Maurice Levermore,
Walter Staplehill, John Blackhall, Richarde Prestwoode, John
Wolcot, Thomas Richardson, Thomas Lambert, Robert Chaffe,
Harrye Maunder, Peter Lake, John Vowell al's Hoker, Eustas
Olyver, Thomas Marshall, William Chapell, William Tryvett,
Edwarde Lymett, Thomas Prestwoode, Nicholas Martyn,
Thomas Spicer, Hubert Collwill, Michaell German, Richarde
Hasellwoode, William Waye, Assistantes, and to all others
Marchantes Adventurers named and recited in the letters
patentes of their saide Corporacion, as by the same maye appere
and to their successors in the saide Corporacion hereafter. The
Armes and Crest with the supporters in maner as hereafter

ARMS OF THE GUILD.

foloweth, That is to saye, azure A Castell standinge in the poinet wave ij Crownes in chieff gold, upon the helme on a torse golde and azure, A lyons paw gulz holding a grappell golde, the cordes gulz, mantelyd gules dobled argent, supported by a dolphyn argent fynned, tosked and wateled golde, and a porkepygge golde pened sable as more playnly apperyth depicted in this margent. To have and to holde the saide Armes helme and crest with the supporters, to them and to all those of the saide Corporacion and to their successors in the same forevermore. And they it to beare use and shewe in shyldes, banners, standers and otherwyse, to their worshippes at their lybarties and pleasures without impediment lett or interruption of any parson or parsons. In witness wherof the saide Clarencieulx Kinge of Armes have signed these pesentes with my hande and sett thereunto as well the seale of myne office as the seale of myne armes. Geven at London the fyrst daye of Julye in the yeare of oure Lorde God 1560 In the seconde yeare of the reigne of our sovereigne ladye Elizabeth by the grace of God Queene of Englande Ffraunce and Irlande &c.

The Statutes and Ordinances of the saide Societie devised by the Governor Consultes and Companye.

The Governor to cause his companye to be sommoned

INPRIMIS That the Governo' and Consultes when so ever they shall see or have any occasion to call their Brethren or Companye shall appointe the Bedell or warners of this Societie to geve to everye suche parson or parsons a sufficient warning or sommons.

Every of the Societie warned to geve his due attendance.

ITEM That every one of the said Societie so somoned shall geve his trewe attendance and dyligence at the tyme prefyxed unlesse he have a reasonable excuse and a lawfull cause to the contrarye, or at the furthest within one halfe hower after that the Governo' and Consultes be com to syt in place, upon the forfect of ffower pence, and yf he so somoned come not at all then to paye for his absence syx pence, except a reasonable and lawfull excuse to the contrary.

Every one of the Companye to geve his due reverence to the Governor.

ITEM That every one of the saide companye when he cometh to the place or halle of assemble shall fyrst geve his dewe reverence to the Governo' and Consultes for the tyme being, and then to take his seate or place accordinglye and lykewyse shall reverentlie salute theim where and when soever he shall mete the saide Governo'.

ITEM That none of the saide companye shall propone any matter to be commoned in the haule or place of assemble, but he fyrste do reverentlie stande upp and so to saye his mynde.

STATUTES AND ORDINANCES.   15

None to interrupt an other telling his tale.
ITEM: That none of the said societie shall interrupte any other of the Copanye as longe as he is telling of his tale, Nether yet to be talkatyve or yangeling upon payne to paye for everye such offence two pence.

The Governor to have a hammer.
ITEM: that the Governo' having a small hammer in his hande, made for the purpose, when he will have scilence to be hadd, shall knocke the same upon the Borde, and who so ever do talke after the seconde stroke, to paye without redempcion: two pence.

No acte to be made without the more part of the Assistaunce.
ITEM: that the Governo' and Consultes shall make no acte nor ordynaunce for this Societie unless there be twentie or the more parte of the Assistante Counsell ioyned with theim besides other of the Companye.

Every one to bringe his Brother to Church at Buryall.
ITEM: whensoever any of the saide Company shall happen to be maried or buryed, that then every one of his Brethren being lawfullie somoned shall geve his attendance to the Governo' and Consultes, and bring the partie in decent order to the Churche upon payne of every suche defaulcte to paye vi*d*: unless he have a lawful excuse to the contrarie or lycence.

ITEM: that no parson be taken or admytted to be a freeman of this Societie unless he be shortlie made free of the liberties of the Citie of Exon, wch is to saye within one moneth.

| The eldest sone to have the pryveledge of this freedome. | ITEM that the eldest sone of every ffreeman or ffreewoman of this Societie after his deathe shall have the pryvelege of the freedome of this Companye accordinge to the auncient liberties of the Citie, paying only the ffees of the house and Companye So that he do frequent and exercyse the trade of marchaundise. |

| Every one free in this Companye to be resident within the Citie | ITEM that no person admytted to the ffreedome of this Companye shall enioye the same unless he be residunt, abyding and dwelling within the liberties of the citie or countie of Exon. |

| Every Apprentice to be free of this Companye | ITEM that the Apprentice of every ffreeman or ffreewoman of this Companye shall be admytted to the ffreedome of this Societie paying onelye the ordynarie ffees: Yf he bringe in his indentures and prove that he hathe well and trewlie served his maistere or maisteres being free of this Companye, by the space of seven yeares. |

| The ffees of every freeman sworn. | ITEM who so ever be admytted to the ffreedome of this Companye shall at the taking of his othe paye or cause to be paied the some of fyve shillinges of lawfull money for the ffees: which shalbe distributed and devided in maner and forme folowinge That ys to the Governo' of the saide Companye for the tyme beinge viij$d$, to the ffower Consultes to every of them vj$d$, to the Clerke viij$d$, to the Beddle viij$d$, and the residue being vij$d$ to the common cofer or to the Treasurer to the use of the Societie |

STATUTES AND ORDINANCES.   17

The ffees of every ffreeman sworne

ITEM yf any parson or parsons being free of this Companye do dye having any apprentises whose yeares and termes ys not then expired nor determyned Yf thexecutors or assignes of suche parson then dedd cannot iustlye clayme the service of suche apprentice or apprentices by lawe during the residue of the terme to come, That then the Governo' and Consultes of this Companye for the tyme being shall by their dyscrecions put and set suche apprentise or apprentises to any other ffree parson of this Company whome he shall serve during suche tyme and terme as is yet to come of his ap-prentishode

Touchinge Apprentises.

ITEM Yf any being free of this companye whose apprentise or apprentises have or shall have by indentures or otherwyse by covenaunt, any libertie of occupie under their M^{rs} any goodes or stocke by the trade of merchaundise before the tyme of their prentishode expired, That every suche apprentice before he doo soo occupie the saide trade shalbe fyrst presented by his M^r before the Governo' and Consultes of this Companye, and to make ffyne for suche his occupyeing as they shall thinke good with thadvyse of the Assistant Counsell, And thus shall he doo by hymselfe or some other everye yeare at the election of the newe Governo' and Consultes or very shortlie after : And every apprentise wch doeth contrary to this order for every tyme shall lose and forfect xls to be levied upon all his goodes wheresoever it may be founde orelles to be commytted to pryson : by the discrecion of the Governo' and Consultes for the tyme being.

E

ITEM That every apprentise who shall during his apprentischode occupye any stocke to his owne use shall from tyme to tyme paye the Towne custome as other foryners do.

<small>Every one free of this Companye to aske leave of the Governor before he commence any lawe ageinst any freeman of this Company.</small>

ITEM Yf any debate or controversie about any accompte or otherwyse doo happen betwene any of this Companye, That then the same variance to be revealed to the Governo' and Consultes of the Companye, who according to their discrecions may take ffurther order therein for the endying and appeasing of the same, which yf they cannot redresse : That then it shalbe lawfull for the saide parties to procede in wager and tryall of lawe : Orelles not.

THE OTHE TO BE MYNISTRED TO THE GOVERNOR AND CONSULTES OF THE COMPANYE OF THE MARCHANTES ADVENTURERS OF THE CITIE OF EXON FOR THE YEARE BEINGE. BY THE MAIOR OF THE SAID CITIE.

Ye shall sware That ye shalbe good and trewe to oure moste Sovereigne Ladye the Quene's Highness by the Grace of God Quene of Englande Fraunce and Ireland defender of the faithe etc and to her heirs and successors Kings and Quenes of Englande and ye shall upholde and maynteine all articles and grauntes comprysed in your Charter of Marchantes Adventurers and all other ordynaunces and statutes of ye same societie to the uttermost of your power for this present yeare following. Youe shall as often as is made require cause to be called together ye Companye or as many as shall be required to sit and consulte for the reformation of all complayntes or wrongs committed or done by any of your Companye or others. Ye shall see to the uttermost of your powres that none of your Companye do sell deccitful wares or use any faulse weightes or measures. Ye shall geve in charge at your Assembles to all and every of your Companye that they be of an honeste and discrete behaviour to the good ensamble of all the Quene's subjects. Ye shall dyscretlye and circumspectlie make and order such statutes and ordynances amonge yourselves as shall not be hurtful repugnante nor prejudiciall to the Lawes of this realme nor the common welthe of this Citie of Exon. Ye shall with favor and gentleness use offenders putting aparte all cruelness and dyspleasure. All and singles these statutes ye shall well and truelie kepe. So helpe ye God.

The Othe to be Mynystred to the Threasurer.

Ye shalbe trewe and faithfull to oure Sovereigne Ladye Elizabeth by the grace of God Quene of Englande &c and to her heires and successors Kinges and Quenes of Englande, and to the Governo' Consultes and Companye of this Merchantes Adventurers of the Citie of Exon as the Threasurer of the saide Societie : Youe shall upon all reasonable somons be attendante upon the saide Governo' and Consultes unles youe have a lawfull excuse : You shall saffely and trewelie kepe and governe all suche goodes money or somes of money and all other receites which shall or maye come to youre hands to the use of the Companie of the forsaide Marchauntes Adventurers : Youe shall aske trewe allowance of all suche charges and expences as youe have or shalbe at, during the tyme being Threasurer of this Companye. Youe shall at thende of the yeare within one moneth after the syx day of August next commyng make youre accompte before the Governo' Consultes and Companye : And all suche goodes as shall then remayne in youre handes at the determynacion of your accompte youe shall then and there deliver into the handes of the Threasurer then being : All whiche articles and all others hereafter to be devysed touching your office you shall well and trewlie kepe and observe :

THE OTHE TO BE MYNSTERED TO EVERY ONE WHICH IS AND SHALL BE MADE FREE OF THE COMPANYE OF THE MARCHANTES ADVENTURES OF THE CITIE OF EXESTER.

YOUE shall swere youe shalbe good and trewe to our Soveregine Ladye the Quenes Highnes Ladye Elizabeth by the Grace of God Quene of England Ffrance and Irlande defender of the faithe &c and to her heires and successors Kinges and Quenes of Englande: You shalbe obedient to the Maior of this Citie of Exon and to the Governor and Consultes of this Companye of the Marchauntes Adventurers: You shall mainteine as muche as in youe shall lye all the liberties of the same being not preiudiciall nor hurtfull to the liberties of the Citie Youe shall come to the election of every new Governo' and Consulte Youe shalbe contributorie to all maner of charges, after your liabilitie, as youe shalbe taxed with all by the Governo' Consultes and Assistaunte Councele of this Companye: Youe shall not coulo' any foreyne goodes wherebye the Quenes highnes may at any tyme lose any parte of her custome or which maye be preiudiciall to the custome of the Citie: Yf youe shall knowe any maner of parson or parsones being not free of this Companye to transporte any marchandize growen or made oute of this realme of England or domynions of the same, contrarye to the graunte made by the Quenes highnes to the Marchantes Adventurers of this Citie of Exon, you shall furthwithe geve knowledge and warnying thereof to the Governo' and Consultes of this Companye for the tyme being, or to one of theim at the leaste: Yf you shall knowe any unlawfull assembles conventicles or conspiracies made ageyne the Quene's peace youe shall geve knowledge of the same to Mr. Maio^r of this Citie or the Governo' and Consultes of this Companye for the tyme being: Yf any variance or controversie shall at any tyme happen to

F

ryse betwene any youre brethren of this Companye, youe shall put your helping hand for the pacifienge and asswaging of the same : Youe shall sharplie rebuke and reprove bothe within this realme and also in the parties beyonde the seas, all mens sarvantes or factors of this Companye yf at any tyme it shalbe your chaunce to see or knowe theim negligentlie ryottoslie or dysceytfullie to handle their maisters busynes and goodes   That with all spede convenyent youe open and reveale suche their mysbehavio^r and evel lyving and dealing to their masters, and not to conceale the same in any wyse   Youe shall not dysclose the secret talke communed by the Governo^r and Consultes or any of theim to be kept secret, which may be hurtfull to the said Companye. You shall observe kepe and obeye all suche goode actes and ordynances as be, or hereafter shalbe, made and devised by the Governo^r Consultes and Assistante Counsell of this Companye for the good goverment and preservacion of the same Companye in all poinctes and articles as moche as in youe shall or may lye : All and singuler these articles, youe shall well and trulie observe and kepe as a freeman of this Companye, as longe as you shall contynue a freeman of the same : So helpe youe God : etc.

THE GUILD HALL.

John Hoker,
A.D 1601 æt. 76.
"Post mortem vita"

An Elizabethan Guild of the City of Exeter.

In the year 1549 this fair City of Exeter endured for a whole summer month the horrors of a siege. Beset by rebel fanatics, whose minds were affected, Hoker says, owing " to the sun being in Cancer and the midsummer moon at full," and who numbered partisans and sympathizers within the gates superior to the loyal and well affected, the Mayor and principal citizens had enough to do to hold their own, and prevent the enemy from taking possession of the City.

Lord Russell who had been sent down by the king to suppress the rebellion was at this time at Honiton, " in an agony and of a heavy cheer," prevented from moving for want of men and money. It chanced then that three Merchants of Exeter—John Bodlie, Thomas Prestwood, and John Periam—" understanding of his Lordship's heaviness and grief, did procure such a mass of money" as provided all that was necessary to enable him to march forward, disperse the enemy, and raise the siege: which was accomplished on the 6th August in the same year.

This act on the part of the three Merchants, together with the steadfast loyalty of their brethren within the walls of the City, was not forgotten (direct reference to it being made in the Charter) ten years later, when Elizabeth, who had ascended the throne amid the hopes and joys of the whole nation, granted the Merchants of Exeter that Charter of privileges on which was founded the important Guild of the Merchant Adventurers of the City of Exeter.

The mention of Elizabethan days naturally conjures up names which can never be separated from the history of our country

With these we shall have but little to do, although West countrymen may well be proud of them and should never be weary of the oft-told tale of glory and adventure in which they occupy so conspicuous a position. But there are other names, lost sight of and eclipsed by the brilliance of those surrounded by the strong light of romantic adventure and glorious achievement, which deserve a place in history, at all events, in local history, for they are inseparably connected with the dawn of that industry, that maritime commerce, and that legitimate enterprize which constitute the real greatness of this country.

The policy of Elizabeth early showed itself in an earnest desire to encourage and develop mercantile interests, and although it has been somewhat generally accepted as historical fact that she stimulated the Merchants, by concessions and favors, to amass wealth in order that she might fleece them for the benefit of her favorites, yet, notwithstanding that there may be some foundation for the charge, it may perhaps also be assumed that, considering the great advantages they enjoyed, the Merchants were willing victims and complained very much less than their sympathizers of the present day.

The Charter for the incorporation of the Merchant Adventurers of the City of Exeter trading to France and beyond the seas was granted by Queen Elizabeth within a few months of her accession to the Throne. It is a lengthy document and will be found *in extenso* at the commencement of the volume.

It may be easily imagined, considering the powers and privileges granted, that as the Company grew in strength and influence, a kind of "Imperium in Imperio" would be established, and that the laws of the Guild would become the laws of the City. Indications of this kind show themselves, and in more than one instance the Mayor of the City, although the greatest man in it, found that the Governor of the Company was a greater.

The Merchants were not allowed to take up their privileges

THE GUILD.

Appendix I.

without a struggle. No sooner was the character of the Charter known than the other City Companies, headed by the Tailors, combined to prosecute suits in order to upset it.[1]

Nearly two years of confusion and disturbance ensued which well nigh drove the Citizens to distraction, until the cause of the Merchants, as might have been expected, with the royal determination to uphold it, triumphed. John Hoker, the historian, one of the earliest members of the Guild, acted on the part of the Merchants, and when the settlement was completed unburdened his mind in a lengthy oration to the populace explaining the whole question, which is preserved in his own handwriting in the City Muniment room.

The difficulties which delayed the signing of the Charter having been removed, it was on the 17th June, 1560, as recorded at the foot of the document, "Done by the Queene herself and of the date as aforesaide by authoritie of Parliament."

In the beginning of the same year, seeing an end to their troubles and virtually assured of their privileges, the Merchants assembled and proceeded to establish their Company on a formal basis. John Peter found himself in the Governor's chair, and the names of other officials are duly recorded, including that of Mr. John Buller, Mayor, who was present *ex officio*. The only business before them is the application of three persons for admission to the freedom of the Company— one of them being an "apoticarie"—but they are put back for examination. On a subsequent day they are declared to be "hable ffyt and mete" and are accepted.

The first election day under the Charter was the 6th of August, 1560, and the ceremony took place in the Chapel Chamber of the Guildhall, when Mr. William Hurste was sworn in as the new Governor, and there were forty-three members

---

[1] Hoker's MSS. in the City Muniment room contain a full account of the quarrel and the suits resulting from it.

present. The Courts for some years were chiefly occupied in settling controversies and disputes between the members, and in inflicting fines for breaches of the Charter. A permanent ordinance was adopted at the Courte kept xxvi January, 1561, when it was agreed that the proclamation and order made by the "Lorde Maior of London consernyng the good and honest behaviour of Citizens and Apprentises shalbe put in use by this Companye for the due observation of the same, and have chosen and elected

Mr. Morris Levermore
Mr. John Peter
Thomas Prestwodde
Eustace Olyver
William Trevryth
Robert Cotton
} "To make serche amonge all this Companye, and to geve reporte of their doinges at this side Shroveltide next ensuying."

Some of the old merchants did not at once perceive the advantage of joining the Guild, nor did they think the monopoly would be insisted upon. Mr. John Periam (of whom we shall hear again) was fined twenty marks for trading to France in 1562, not being free of the Company, and neither he nor John Hackewill joined as brethren until ten years afterwards.

II. John Pyll, who also infringed the rules, was astonished to find a "ffardell of dowlas" seized as a security for any fine that might be inflicted. He ridiculed the idea of paying a fine, and "with scoffinge and tawntinge" demanded that his "ffardell" should be re-delivered together with 13s. 4d. for his charges. An order of committal to the ward-room of the Guildhall however brought him to his senses, and he thought it best to submit and become free of the Company.

Some delinquents not being provided with the necessary means for meeting the fines put in what was called a "paune."

John Perium,
A.D. 1616.

Appendix "XXI Oct. 1561.—At which daye Harry Maunder, being called to pay the iij*l* xviij*s* x*d* which he oweth to this Companye, brought a goblet sylver parcell gylte the foote whereof is broken awaye from it. And the same remayneth in the coffer with the bookes, and lyeth for a gage for the same, untill he bringe the saide money which must be on thisside the nexte Courte: which cupp wayeth xij oz."

"XXVIth Maye 1562.—At which daye a goblett of Harry Maunders waying xij ounces and a halfe praysed at iiij*s* vj*d* the ounce: amounteth in the whole to lvj*s* iij*d* and was solde for the payment of his debt which was iij*l* xviij*s* x*d* So he oweth yet cleare the some of xxij*s* vj*d*."

"XXVth Oct. 1561.—Mr. William Bucknam brought in to this howse a pawne: A goblet sylver parcell gylte for the payment of iiij*l* xiiij*s* iiij*d* which he oweth to this Companye: And he upon his payment to stande to the grace and favo^r of the howse."

"XXVIth Maye 1562.—At which daye also a goblet of Mr. Bucknams which remayned in pawne for iiij*l* xiij*s* iiij*d* was delivered upon hys promyse made That he at his deathe shall and will geve to this Companye the saide goblet waying aboute xiiij oz or some other thinge worthe the same or better."

This William Bucknam or, as Izacke spells it, Buckenam was an Alderman of the City at this time, and was probably the person of the same name who was Mayor in 1541.

The policy of the Guild showed a determination to maintain the strictest discipline; fines were inflicted for non-attendance (xij*d*), and for being late at Court or "his slackness" (vi*d*). Considering that the meetings were called at eight, and sometimes as early as seven o'clock in the morning, it is not to be wondered at that the fines were rather numerous. Some of the members seemed disinclined to submit to being mulcted in this manner, and only yielded on being committed to ward. Severer measures were however necessary, and we find that at the Court

Appendix held 27th March, 1561, confirming fine of xij$d$ for those absenting themselves. The resolution continues:—

"And forasmoche as some of this Companye standing stubborne contemptious and flowte ar to be restrayned with a more severitie: Yt is ordered enacted and decreed That yf any parson or parsons of this Companye being lawfullie somoned and warned to appere before the Governo' Consultes and Companye at any Courte before theim or the more parte of theim to be holden do ffrowardlie or contemptiouslye departe out of the towne without lycence obteyned or being within the Citie do of a lyke frowardnes contempte or dysdeyne absent hym selfe from the saide Courte: That then evry parson so offendynge to paye for this his ffirst contempte and mysbehaviour the some of xs And for the seconde contempte to paye xx$s$ And for the thirde contempte xl$s$ And if he thenceforthe contynewe ffrowarde contemptuose or dysdeynefull to be theane dysmyssed from the saide Companye."

"John Toker, the Bedell, presenteth the names of those who do absent themselves," "in consederation of hys paynes" he is paid 26s 8d per annum. At the General Court of 1562 four persons were committed to ward for not paying their fines, and subsequently a "stresse was taken and brought into Courte of Richard Modetts for his absence at Courte" which was a "tapnett of ffygges." In addition to any punishment, persons not paying their debts at the appointed time are to pay "over and besides" 2d for every shilling owing.

III. There was an imposition called "Average Money," 1d being charged for every tun of wine and for every fardell of cloth shipped inwards or outwards of the port. The proceeds went towards the expenses of the house, but the accounts appear to have been loosely kept and cannot be depended upon. It was only when money was wanted that the Treasurer became extremely active and resorted to stern measures.

Frog Street, (West Quarter).

Appendix   After some years this "average money" was farmed out and brought in at 1*d* £10 or £12 per annum. The rate was doubled and quadrupled before the end of the century.

So little business was doing in 1566 that the Governor and four Consulls elect were not present. The first was ordered to be fined £5, and the others 40s each if they came not to the next Court. They did.

IV.   In August, 1568, the first Lottery instituted in England was supported by the members—sixty-four of whom took up ninety-six shares of 10s. each. Even "John Toker the Bedell" risked his hardly earned 10s. There is no record that any prize was drawn, but it would be a sufficient inducement for the Merchants to subscribe, in the fact that the proceeds or profits of the Lottery were to be devoted to the protection of the coast. A period of stagnation prevailed during the earlier years of the Guild, and it can be accounted for. The close of the war with France brought about a calamity worse than defeat. Our plague-stricken troops returning from Havre de Grace brought with them that terrible scourge. The soldiers dispersing to their own homes, in different parts of the country, spread the infection; and, although the fatal disease does not appear to have reached Exeter until 1569, yet all communication with London and the infected towns was cut off, and the citizens lived in an atmosphere of distrust and suspicion and fear. One may be sure that our merchants did their duty during those terrible times; and if the account of our Treasurer, John Pope, "by reason of the sycknes in Exon" is omitted from the record, it was not from any sense of its falling short in liberality.

V.

There was one undertaking by the Company about this time which deserves notice on account of its historical interest. The carrying trade previous to, and in the early part of Elizabeth's reign, was almost entirely monopolised by the

Appendix Italian and Flemish shipowners. It was the Queen's policy to encourage and develop British maritime interests; directly by concessions and proclamations, and indirectly by granting such charters as the Merchants possessed. Purchas, in his panegyric on the "Mother of England's sea greatnesse," says amongst other things in allusion to this subject, "thou freedst England from Easterlings and Lombards borrowed legs, and taught her not only to stand and goe without helpe but to become helpe to our friends &c."

The state of affairs in Exeter, the year before Elizabeth's accession, is disclosed in a draft answer to a requisition from the Crown, for ships doubly manned and doubly found to go to Calais.

13 *Jan.* 1557. *Draft answer of Merchants of Exeter to Lord Winchester.*

"They cannot execute his orders because no man of the County and City of Exeter hath any ship of his own, nor have any commission to take up ships mariners victuals or any other thing appertaining to ships for the wars out of their own County and City," nor can they borrow money to do it, "bycause of very late and nowe it is yn hand that a great number of men as well within the Cetie of Exeter as yn the Countie of Devon do disburse to the Quene's mat^{ie} by way of lone a great masse of tresure."—*(City Archives)*.

Less than ten years later, fortified with the encouraging influence of an enlightened and patriotic government, our Merchants ventured on an experiment, which, whilst it freed them from dependence upon foreign aid, initiated that maritime enterprize in Devonshire which, not long after, made her pre-eminent in this respect among all counties in the empire.

Appendix The following extracts will explain themselves :—

16 July, 1566. "At this Courte the Governo' Consulls and Companye have taken two shippes to ffreight : one called the Michael of Excester owners of the same Eustace Oliver and Thomas Browne and thother called the Bartlemew of Exmouth owner of the same Roberte Vynton for xl tone apece : to go for velys malaga and ther to take in their ladinge, or a thisside (in resons). And the owner or owners of the shipp to have for every tone of ffreight the some of xlviij$s$ to be paid at the retorne of the same shipp according to the charterpartes thereof to be made. And the said owners have covenanted to make readye the same shipps a thisside the xvth daie of August next : And the Marchauntes laders of the said shipps shalbe also readie by the same daie with their wares, and shipp the same upon payne on hym and every of theim that shall make defaulte to paye dedd freight according to his or their porcions."

" AND further upon conclusion and agreement of the premisses the saide Marchants gave to the owners to every of theim iiij$d$ in ernest, as a goddes peny : which the said owners gave backe ageyne to the Box to the behoffe of the Poore : And farther more the owner and owners of every shipp and barke before named have upon the saide agreement covenaunted and promised to geve to the house at their retorne this voyage the some of xs."

"ALSO at the said Courte the Governo' Consulls and Company have taken a barke to ffreight called the Mary Martyn of Excester, owners thereof Mr. William Hurste, Symon Knight and Thomas Martyn for fortie tonne To goo for Algarbe in Portugal and ther to take in her ladinge in fiygges : And the owners to have for every tonne the some of fyve and fortie shillinges, to be paide at the Barkes retorne accordinge to the charterpartie thereof to be made : And the saide Owners have covenanted to make readie the saide Barke, a thisside the saide xvth daye of August next. And the Marchantes laders of the same Barke shall also be readye by the same daye with their wares and shipp the same, upon payne aforesaide."

Court held 6 August, 1566. "Those which are appointed to take shipping for this yeare have certified at this Courte that they have taken to freight one shipp called the Margaret Carwythen for lx tone : oner thereof Richarde Carwythen : to lade wynes at Juberaltare or Sherys, and the saide owner to have xliijs iiijd for a tone."

VI. "Also they have taken to freight the Christopher of Dartmouth for lx tone, owner thereof John Prouse, to lade wynes at Juberaltare or Sherys : And the saide owner to have xliiijs for a tone and a butt of hollocke for the whole freight."

The Merchants' Company had a Hall of their own in which they elected the Governor and other officers, transacted their business, and dined on election days. This Hall must not be confounded with the Merchants' Hall, the property of the Chamber, which formed a part of the New Inn in High Street, on the site now occupied by Mr. Green's premises, which Hall had more the character of an open market or a place of general resort for the cloth merchants. "Oure haule," the Company's Hall, is frequently alluded to in the minutes, and was well known, although diligent research has failed to trace its precise situation.

The first meetings of the Company were held in the Chapel Chamber of the Guildhall, and it may be inferred that their own Hall, taken on a lease and furnished by them, was not far distant, as the members were summoned by the bell (which still surmounts the Guildhall) of the Chapel of St. George, which formed a portion of the Guildhall premises.

The following extracts from the minutes relate to this part of the subject :—

Bellringing.—18 May, 1587. "At this Courte it is ordered by the whole generalitie that there shalbe yearly paid towardes the ringinge of St. George's Bell the some of tenne shillings, which

Old Houses at West Gate.

Appendix shalbe paid by o' Treasorer so longe as the same bell shalbe orderly runge (and no longer)."

Rent of Hall.—31ˢᵗ March, 1579. "Also at this Courte it is agreed that John Samforde shall have the yerelie rent of iiij*l* for the Marchauntes Haule and the litle howse adjoininge to the same: whereof the Spanish Companye shall paye I*s* by the yeare and Marchauntes Adventurers of Exeter xxx*s*. And also it is agreed that the saide John Samforde shall have v markes for and towardes his charges bestowed in the saide haule."

Courte held 21ˢᵗ Nov. 1587. "Also at the same Court it is agreed that Mr. John Sampforde shall have xl*s* in full and clere discharge of certaine rente dewe by the Spanishe Companie for the Merchauntes Haule, and thereuppon the said Mr. Sampforde hath delivered to this Companie one chest with twoo lockes and keis together with the seelinge bordes, formes, and all other impelmentes remayninge and beinge within o' haule (the glasse only excepted.)"

Lease of Hall.—6 July 1602. "At this Courte Mr. Sampforde for the consideracion of a vi*l* xiij*s* iiij*d* to be paid at the ffeast of S. Michael next doth graunt and lett to this Companie the hall for this Companie which they now use for thirttie yeares from the xxiiij^{th} daie of June last past yf the said John Samforde his wief and John his sonne so long live for a yearlie rent of a iij*l* vi*s* viij*d* quarterly to be paid. And if the said John Sampforde cannot graunte the said lease without a ffine to be levied, then the said John Sampforde is to paie the moitie of the said ffine."

Inventory.—21st daie of November 1587. At this Courte an inventory is exhibited and brought in by Mr. Sampforde, Mr. Bevis and Mr. Applyn of divers goodes and impelmentes apperteyning and belonginge to this Companie which is by order of the house delivered to o' Tresorer Howell as doth hereafter particulerly appere:

Appendix Imprimis One Ansine of taffita sarcenet of yellowe and blewe contg. tenne yardes franged with yellowe and blewe frange.

Item One scarf belonginge to the same for the Ansine bearer of yellowe and blewe franged at the ende with silke frange.

Item One old Ansine of grene silke franged and painted with the Merchauntes Armes.

Item One other Ansine of carnacion and grene silke.

Item A scarf of redd and grene silk for an ansine bearer contg. ij yardes.

Item a scarff of blewe [Levan / leven] taffita contg, neere twoo yardes and half.

Item a drome, a case of buckram, and two dromestickes.

Item two staves for ansines.

Item a tabell of the Merchauntes armes.

Item xx lether buckets.

Item a ladder and a iron crowke which is to be repaired.

Item a faire tabell borde with a frame twoo ffair table bords of ferr iiij tressels to beare them eight longe formes and two shorter formes with drilled leggs.

Item two bynches fixed to the walles.

Item the seelinge aboute the table and bynches to the same.

Item halfe a dossen of grene kersey quishions.

Item a olde carpet of greene contg. twoo yards quarter.

Item a mallet for the Governo' to knocke.

Item one mape.

Item one chest with twoo locks and keys.

23 August 1593. Quishions increased to a dozen also a tabell of actes made and devised by the Companie.

Item one other newe carpet cont.

Item a shorte forme.

Item ffower joyned stooles and two foote stooles.

Item a blacke boxe and exemplification of the previe seale for mittigatinge of custome upon kersaies."

Walter Borough.
A.D. 1626 æt. 72.

Appendix It may be interesting to know what manner of men these were who composed this Guild. Hoker says they were the "chiefest and wealthiest men in the city." Fortunately we can go further than this and obtain a nearer acquaintance with them. The names of some of them are historical, the names of many are engraven on our memories by the charities they founded, and the features of a few are still preserved to us in their portraits which hang on the walls of the Council Chamber of the Guildhall. Let us take these latter first. There is—

VII.
John Peryam, son of John Periam, twice Mayor, and one of the three Merchants of Exeter who in 1549, on the memorable occasion alluded to at the commencement, supplied Lord Russell with the means which enabled him to raise the siege of Exeter. You can read his character in his countenance—resolute, energetic, imperious, a man who would have his way, and whom one would not care to thwart. He refused to accept the Governorship of the Company in 1585, because "he did not minde to remayne in this Cittie as an inhabitant, but to dwell at London where his howshold doth now remayne, and shewing other causes that he must nedes be absent from this Cittie for this yere or more." One of the "other causes" doubtless being that a residence near his brother, Sir William, the Lord Chief Baron of the Exchequer, was advantageous in more ways than one. He was, however, subsequently twice elected Governor—on certain conditions and protestations, which he insisted upon—and twice Mayor of the City. He was knighted, and died at his seat near Crediton. He left by will—amongst numerous other benefactions—£1000 to be lent to five persons, being freemen of the Company, "especially to them of the meaner sort," £200 to each for three years.

Walter Borough, Mayor in 1610. A fine, grave, handsome man, with Jewish features, closely cut hair and well trimmed

Appendix beard. One is almost prompted to say, with Salarino, in looking at that countenance.

> "Your mind is tossing on the ocean;
> There, where your argosies with portly sail,
> Like signiors and rich burghers on the flood,
> Or, as it were, the pageants of the sea,
> Do overpeer the petty traffickers."

He was Mayor of the City on two occasions in the years 1610 and 1621, and his name is still recorded on the list of our charitable benefactors.

VIII. Loyal William Hurst, the first elected Governor of the Company, and five times Mayor of Exeter—sufficient evidence of his amiable, courteous, and generous character if it were not written in his every feature. His son, who inherited his wealth, was too great a man to join the Guild, and is alluded to in a somewhat sarcastic minute, as Mr. William Hurst, Esquire. William Hurst's name is still remembered by us in connexion with the almshouses now situate in Spiller's Street. The original houses, which he built and endowed, occupied the site, just without the walls, where Northernhay Place now stands. (John Lant, another member of the Guild, further endowed these almshouses).

Two Latin lines on William Hurst's portrait demonstrate that he was of humble origin and was not ashamed of it—

> "Non mihi lingua datur; qua possim dicere nomen:
> Qualis eram: paucis: versa tabella notat."

One naturally refers to the back of the picture and finds— NOTHING!

Laurence Atwill, founder of the Almshouses which bear his name, and grandson of that Atwill who was five times Mayor of Exeter under four successive Sovereigns—

> "He saw five princes which the sceptre bore,
> Of these he was a magistrate to four."—*Vilvayne*.

William Hurst,
A.D. 1568 æt. 96.

THE GUILD.

Appendix Joan Tuckfield, in the uncomfortable dress of the period, but with jewelled head-dress and golden girdle to show her quality. Her husband was a member of the Guild, and she was a benefactor to it, as well as to the City in other ways.

John Hoker—who does not know John Hoker? without whom Exeter would scarcely have had a published history. City Chamberlain, Burgess in Parliament, industrious, observant historian, his name should be a household word with us. The bright, intelligent face shows advanced life, but there is fire still in the eyes, and energy in the general expression. He is taken in the official robes, and wears a hat which is not only hideous, but enviously covers the best part of what must have been a good head.

The portrait of Hugh Crossing, the founder of St. John's Hospital, is fitly placed in the Grammar School, to the Trustees of which it was presented by the Corporation. Hugh Crossing was a member of the Guild, and probably became governor early in the seventeenth century after the time to which the records extend. He was Mayor of the city in 1609, and again in 1620, and died in 1621 at the early age of 55.

The portrait of Nicholas Spicer, which was formerly in in the Council Chamber, has been removed elsewhere. The name of the founder of Spicer's Charity is not, however, likely to be soon lost sight of. He was a member of the Guild, as were his brothers Thomas, William, and Christopher, each Governor in his turn. Then we find the names of Thomas Prestwood, who died during his Mayoralty, and Thomas Walker once Governor and twice Mayor, who left by will towards endowing a free Grammar Shool £400. Also Simon Knight, John Hele, William Martin, George Smyth (who was afterwards knighted), John Prouse and Thomas Martin; these all served as Members of Parliament for the City; and we meet with such familiar names as Buckenam

Appendix Follett, Geare, Ellacott, Yarde, Buller, Blackalle, Chaffe, Peryman, and Spurway. Of forty Governors in the reign of Queen Elizabeth, twenty-five were Mayors of the City—five thrice and three twice—sometimes holding both offices at the same time.

Ignatius Jurden, who in King James' time, had become a great merchant of Exeter. He petitioned the King through the Bishop for the better observance of the Lord's Day, being dissatisfied with the "Royal Book of Sports," which enjoined that the people might indulge in lawful recreation after Divine Service. His interference, however, so angered the King that he declared he would hang the fellow. He was one of the burgesses for the City in Parliament in 1624. It is recorded to his credit that when the plague visited Exeter with severity in the year 1625, creating such consternation that the Mayor and all the principal inhabitants fled from the City, he alone, acting as deputy Mayor, remained firmly at his post.

John Hackwill or Hakewell, merchant of Exeter. His eldest son, William, took his degree of M.A. at Oxford, was bred to the law, became a Master in Chancery and one of the Governors of Lincoln's Inn. He served in several Parliaments, wrote many learned works, and was executor of his kinsman, Sir Thomas Bodley. Another son, George, born in the parish of St. Mary Arches in 1598, was elected a Fellow of Exeter College, Oxford, and became Archdeacon of Surrey and Rector of Worcester College. He acquired great reputation by his writings, which were distinguished by their breadth and liberality of sentiment.

The family of Martyn or Martin—spelt in both ways indiscriminately—was a notable one in connexion with the Guild. There appear to have been three brothers, Nicholas, William and Thomas. Nicholas, the eldest, was twice Mayor of Exeter, and twice Governor, but he survived his last election as Governor only six months—his brother William filling the vacant chair for

Hugh Crossing.
Taken in 1621, Aged 55.

Appendix the remainder of the term of office. Nicholas was evidently a wealthy man and a bold successful merchant. He was the first to join in any proposed venture and usually held the largest stake in it. He was a large contributor to the relief of the poor and to other local objects. Seldom any important business went forward without his having something to do with it either as adviser or suitor. He left two sons, his exors, William and Nicholas—the latter was admitted a freeman of the Company in 1599. William, born in 1562, entered Pembroke College, Oxford, 1579, and afterwards studied the law at the Inns of Court. He was made Recorder of Exeter in 1605, and was in good favor with the Court, until he wrote his "History of twenty Kings of England," which mightily offended King James. He was the author of several other learned works, and was a man of considerable literary attainments. The Company appointed him their standing Counsel, and from the liberality displayed towards him and from other evidence, "our Councellor," as he is called, must have been a great favourite.

IX. William Martyn the elder, twice Mayor, was twice elected Governor. He appears to have been the equal of his brother Nicholas in wealth and enterprise. During his second mayoralty he disbursed from his own resources £305 in obtaining a mitigation of customs' duties on woollen cloths. This was a large sum of money in those days. He had two sons, Thomas, a member of the Guild, and Mayor in 1612. Richard, the eldest, born in 1570, went to Pembroke College (whither his cousin had preceded him) as Gentleman Commoner in 1585. He signally distinguished himself at College, and removed to the Inner Temple in 1588; became eminent in his profession, and was returned to Parliament in 1601. He was reckoned one of the most accomplished and witty men of his age, and so charmed the King that he made him Recorder of London in 1618.

H^2

Appendix X.

The third brother, Thomas, joined the Guild in 1566, and was Governor in 1577.

Another of the name, and probably of the same family—John—was admitted by a special Act on the election day, 1597, in consideration of important services rendered in a law suit which the Company were parties to.

John Davie or Davye, once Governor and thrice Mayor. His first mayoralty (and he was Governor of the Company the same year) was distinguished by a feast so magnificent, given in honor of the exiled King of Portugal, as to be thought worthy of historical record. He made a considerable fortune in merchandise, lived in Mary Arches parish, where he built and endowed Almshouses, and in the Church is still to be seen his monument with the following inscription :—

> "This marble monument and fading brass
> Might have been spared, for neither needed was,
> To stand a register to Davies name;
> Who, living, did erect a fairer fame,
> And far more lasting : Whose foundation
> Was firmly grounded on the corner stone :
> Whose bar was faith; whose pillars piety ;.
> And whose engravings, works of charity.
> Then let the dead trust to a dying tomb;
> But how can death in Davie find a room ?
> Whose soul in heaven alive doth aye remain
> Whose works on earth so many lives maintain."

His grandson John was created a baronet in 1641, the title being continued to the present day, and now borne by the respected family at Creedy park, Crediton.

In Mary Arches street and parish were some of the best private residences in the city, as we may infer from the records on the old monuments in the Church. Isacke (page 119) also informs us that a commission appointed to try one Jordan for high treason sat in trial at the house of John Croston, Register, in St. Mary Arches lane. The reader may, on inspection of

Lawrence Atwill,
A.D. 1588 æt. 77.

Appendix the map, form his own conclusion as to the exact spot where John Davye's house was situate. The following extract from the City Records may in some measure help him:

"The Chamber to John Davye, 23rd September, 1591, grant of two stables and gardens in Saint Mary Arches lane, between the said lane on the west, the highway next the city walls from Northgate to Friernhay on the north, the stables and garden of one Yorke on the east, and the gardens and stables of the Chamber on the south, which stables are now in the tenure of the said John Davye; rent reserved, 12s. With a proviso that the said John Davye, after the death of himself and Margaret his wife, shall bestow the premises to the good of the poor of Exeter."

Davye's almshouses, erected in pursuance of the proviso, are still remaining, on the exact spot where the stables referred to were situated, viz., in Bartholomew street, at the corner of Mary Arches street. The door at the entrance to the courtlage of the almshouses bears the initials "J. D." and the year 1592.

Appendix

GOVERNORS OF THE GUILD.

A.D.		MAYOR.
1559.	John Peter	... 1557 1562 1575
1560.	John Hurst	... 1561 1524 1535 1545 1561
1561.	John Mydwynter	
1562.	Morris Levermore	1564
1563.	Robert Mydwynter	
1564.	Eustace Olyver	
1565.	Symon Knight	... 1570
1566.	William Chapell	... 1569 1579
1567.	George Peryman	... 1577
1568.	Thomas Richardson	... 1566
1569.	Nicholas Martyn	.. 1574 1585
1570.	William Tryvett	... 1573
1571.	Robert Chaffe	... 1688 1576
1572.	Thomas Prestwood	... 1576 died
1573.	Thomas Bruarton	... 1571 1580
1574.	John Blackaller	
1575.	John Peter	
1576.	John Pope (d.) Eustace Olyver	
1577.	Thomas Martyn	1581 (1618 ?)
1578.	William Martyn	1590 1600 1602
1579.	Philipp Yarde	
1580.	John Hutchyns	
1581.	Harry Ellacott	
1582.	John Levermore	
1583.	Michaell Germyne	1582 1591

THE OLD BUTCHER ROW, EXETER.

GOVERNORS OF THE GUILD.

Appendix	A.D.		MAYOR.
	1584. John Davye	...	1584 1594 1604
	1585. John Peryam, refused; Thomas Chapell, appointed		
	1586. George Smyth	...	1586 1597 1607 (knighted)
	1587. John Peryam	...	1587 1599
	1588. Nicholas Spicer	...	1592 1603
	1589. Thomas Spicer	...	1593
	1590. John Chappell	...	1595
	1591. John Howell		
	1592. John Sandforde		
	1593. Henry Hull	...	1605
	1594. Richard Bevis	...	1602 (d.)
	1595. Thomas Walker	...	1601
	1596. Richard Dorchester the elder	...	1606
	1597. Christopher Spicer		
	1598. Nicholas Martyn (d.)		
	1599. (27th March) John Peryam, Mayor		
	1599. William Martyn		
	1600. William Spicer		
	1601. John Ellacott		

These are the men we should meet with could we transport ourselves backwards to the Exeter of three hundred years ago. But should we recognize the city itself? The city scarcely extended beyond the walls; Southernhay, a ditch and a dreary waste; St. Sidwell's parish comprising a few scattered houses, and St. David's even less. An inn stood where still swings the sign of the "Valiant Soldier," and between that and Larkbeare House were scarce half-a-dozen small houses; whilst on the other side, the monastery of the Grey Friars was the only building between the Southern gate and the open country and river.

Two or three cottages, beyond the walls, marked the way

Appendix to the Wynard's hospital, the last of the buildings on the Magdalen road, with the exception of the isolated Lazar house in the ditch just beyond.

Within the city, on the spot occupied by Bedford Circus, stood Bedford House, the princely residence of the Earl of Bedford. The main entrance was from High street, through what is now known as Bedford street, across Catherine street, and under the massive gateway into the spacious quadrangle. The grounds, as nearly as possible, comprised the space included between Egypt and old Post Office lanes, Catherine street and the city wall. This is classic ground. Here, on Midsummer eve, at three o'clock of the afternoon, each member of the Guild was required to bring so many men with harness, arms and furniture, to set forth the

XI. Queen's Watch—the annual review, as we should call it, of the Civic Guard. John Davie and five others were at one time officers in command, and twelve members were "Whysselers to goo with the watchè and kepe them in araye," aided no doubt by the big "drome."

Here, the Lady Elizabeth Russell daughter of the Earl was given in marriage to the Earl of Bath,[1] on which occasion the

XII. whole City yielded itself up to festivity, and high jinks were played on Southernhay. On this occasion as on all others our Guild was ever ready. It was resolved that one hundred and five calyvers, thirty-four corsletts, and five almon ryvets—these latter for the Captains—with the requisite number of men in armour " shall be provided for a muster or shewe to be sync before the Right Honorable Lorde therle of Bedforde," and " that this Companye shall provide for everie calyver one pounde of the best corne pouther that may be gotten."

> " Such as fear the report of a caliver worse than a struck fowl or a hurt wild duck."—1 *Henry IV.*, Act 4, Sc. 2.
> " Put me a caliver into Wart's hand".—2 *Henry IV.*, Act 3, Sc. 2.

[1] 7th August, 1582.

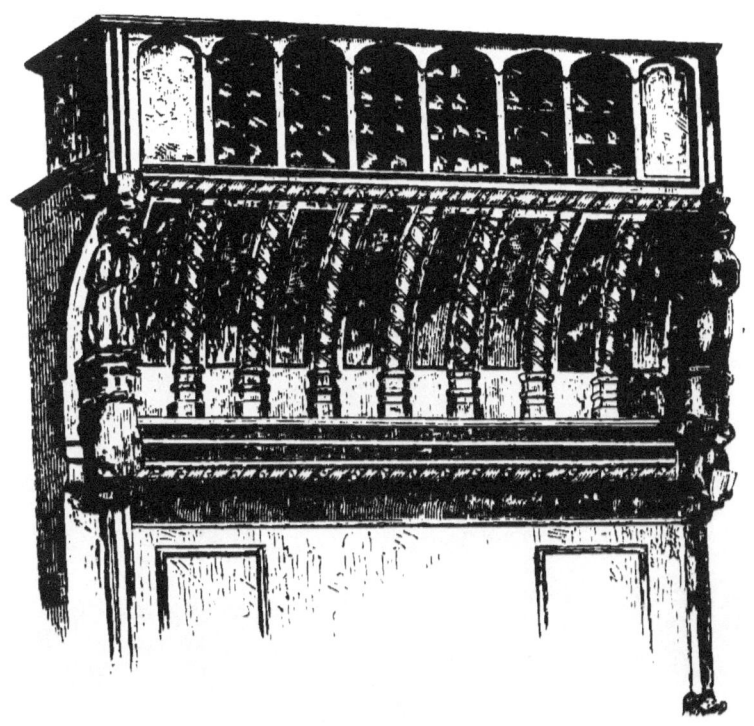

No. 46, High Street.

Appendix   This Earl of Bath resided at Tawstock Court near Barnstaple; and in the diary of Philip Wyot, Town Clerk of Barnstaple (1586 to 1608), edited by Mr. J. R. Chanter, we find constant reference to the family, as his lordship took a prominent part in public affairs. The following extracts from the diary may not be without interest:

"xi March, 1587. Lorde Fitzwarren, son and heire of Lorde Bath, died at Tawstock suddenly but xvi months old."

"15 August, 1587. This day Ld. Bath's son was xtened called Robert Godfar, Sr Richd Greynfylde for Ld Chancellor, Sir Willicm Mown for the E. of Essex, Lady Denys for the old Countes of Bedforde."

"1605. On Palm Sunday, 24 daye of March, dyed at Tawstock, the Countes of Bath, and that night following she was buryed, but the solemnization of her funeral was deferred until some tyme afterwards."

"The Monday beyinge the vith day of May, 1605, was the funeral of the late Elizabeth Countes of Bath solempnized at Tawstock, there came down from London three deputie harolds of armes, the principal mourner was the young lady Frances Bowchier, and there were viii other murners of the poorer sort of the same psh.; Mr. Saunders, the Earl of Bath's Chaplayne did preach that day; much meate and drinke eate and drank at Tawstock Court, all the poor had iij$d$ a piece and loaf of bread."

Between Egypt lane and the Cathedral was the town house of the Abbots of Buckfastleigh (now occupied by Mr. Dawson) and the Archdeaconry residence, both structures remaining to the present day.

Bampfylde House, north of Bedford circus, still exists, and its general plan can be easily traced. The small quadrangle in Bampfylde street, formerly Raden lane, into which the windows looked remains almost unaltered. In the year 1769, the Duke of Bedford, escaping from the fury of the populace—incensed at

Appendix his supposed consent to a secret article in a treaty with France —found a refuge in this quadrangle. The garden belonging to the house was on the opposite side the way, where Pedrick's stables now stand. There are fine specimens of carved work existing, and the ceilings are in the elaborate style of the time. A grand old mantelpiece belonging to the dining hall was removed some years since to Poltimore House, but it dates from nearly half a century subsequent to the time we are writing of.

Perhaps one of the oldest rooms in Exeter is that used as an office by Messrs Harris and Wreford, in Gandy street. The royal arms over the chimney-piece are those of Elizabeth; on the left side are the arms of Roger Mallock, Mayor of Exeter, 1636, and on the other the arms of the Merchant Adventurers, of which Guild he was presumably Governor during his Mayoralty. The carved wainscot and cornice were probably added about the time of his mayoralty. The sumptuous decoration and expensive workmanship seen in these, as well as in the Tucker's Hall in Fore street hill, are excellent specimens of the period, and are evidences of the wealth and prosperity which abounded during the latter years of Elizabeth's reign, and throughout that of her successor.

The best parts of the city in those days were Preston street, Coombe street, St. Mary Arches parish, the east end of High street, Gandy street, and Paul street. There was a fine house also by Jan's Cross in Gandy street, occupied, no doubt, by one of our city merchants, and subsequently by Gandy, who gave his name to the street. In St. Mary Arches street, Pancras lane, Goldsmith street, we have specimens of the main streets of the period, probably little altered as to width, but having no longer the heavy, projecting gables thrust out, so that opposite neighbours could shake hands from their windows.

CHIMNEY-PIECE IN MALLOCK'S HOUSE, GANDY STREET.

CORNER OF NORTH STREET.

Appendix

> "By this, where houses, whelving houses meet,
> And vault with beetle-brows a shelving street,
> Where stout St. Peter, on the corner stall
> Props the impending edifice from fall."—*Mobiad, Canto* 4, *p.* 72.

The private houses had no windows in the lower story facing the street. The approach was through a gateway which led to a quadrangle whereon opened the windows. Sometimes a square of houses was built facing inwards towards an open space, the only entrance being through a gateway, which was carefully secured at night. These precautions were necessary in days when street lamps and watchmen were unknown.

High street, with its picturesque gables, quaint buildings, and windowless shops, extended nearly, without a break, from the East to the West gate.

At the "Quatre Voix" stood the conduit which distributed the water brought from the springs of St. Sidwell's. Northgate street, on the one hand, and what is now known as South street on the other, were scarcely passable except for foot passengers and packhorses. The first part of South street, on the left, entering from the main street, was known as Cook's row: proceeding through it we should have seen St. George's Church on the right, intruding far upon the roadway; a little further down, on the opposite side, was the College kitchen, with the Yarn market in front of it, and, beyond, the extensive premises of the Bear Inn, surmounting Bell hill. Continuing our way to the South gate and passing through, if we turned sharply to the right, down the narrow path between the inner and XIII. outer defences—now indicated by Little Quay lane—we should have found ourselves outside the Water gate, with the store house adjoining, rented by the company from John Sampforde, at 6s 8d a year, for the purpose of storing the wood, which every winter was given away to the poor.

Hoker says that, long before his time, vessels came to this Water gate on the top of the spring tide, but that St. James's

Appendix wear and St. Leonard's (Trew's) wear then stopped the tidal waters. Goods were transported in barges from the craft which lay at anchor in Countess wear pool, through the canal or "New Cut" as it was called, to King's Arms sluice and the landing place near the Custom house. A century later the canal was continued to about a mile above Topsham, opening on the river by Trenchard's[1] sluice, which was done away with when the extension to Turf was carried out in 1830.

It may not be out of place here to record the indirect connexion of the company with a work, which would naturally be of vital importance to the merchants, viz., the shipway from the navigable Exe to the Quay. In Oliver's "History of Exeter" there is an account of the haven or canal, derived from a most carefully prepared memoir by the late Mr. P. C. De la Garde. From this we find that in the autumn of 1566 the first canal or water-course, constructed by John Trewe, was open for the navigation of vessels. It extended from a little below Countess wear bridge to Exeter quay, but being only three feet in depth, the largest vessels (if they may be called so) which could pass through did not exceed sixteen tons burthen.

On 6 September, 1574, we find in the city records that John Trewe, in consideration of £229 and a yearly rent of £30, releases 'all that the new haven or watercourse with the appurtenances uppon or neere the ryver of Exe' and all his interest therein, to the Mayor, Bayliffs, and Commonalty of Exeter; a reciprocal indemnity against liability in respect thereof being granted by the chamber.

The absence of any allusion to the canal in the minutes of the company suggests the inference, that they were content to leave the matter in the hands of the chamber, or that they had

---

[1] Mr. Francis Davy, of Topsham, remembers entering the canal in a vessel through Trenchard's sluice. The gates were sometimes opened at ebb tide, and the water as far as Double locks allowed to flow out in order to scour the channel of the river.

THE WATER GATE (EXTERIOR).

GOVERNORS OF THE GUILD. 49

Appendix XIV. not acquired such a position as would warrant interference. It is not until 1577 that there is any reference to the subject, and then only with respect to the charges exacted at Topsham, which probably were retained as vested rights, and became extremely onerous when the Exeter quay and canal dues were superadded.

" 10 Julie, 1577. At this Courte the Governor, Consulls, and Companye, whose names are hereunder wryten, Did take order and agree that John Samforde a freeman of this Companye shoulde ride to London and there to be their Deputie to deale for them and in their behalf accordinge to his discrecion with Mr. Stubbes, as touchinge the cranage, wharffage, selerage, and portage of all thinges belonginge and apperteyninge to the Bayliffweke of Topsham and to the ryver of Exmouth. And that hee shall have paied hym in hande at his goinge upp by John Davye, Treasurer of this Companye, v^{li} towards his charges. And whatsoever some or somes of money that hee shall disburse laye oute over and besides whether it be to the said Stubbes or in consideration of the graunte of the premisses or otherwise it shalbe allowed and paid hym or his assignes at his retorne home or upon his bill at any time when the same shalbe demanded. And unto this all and everie the said parties hereunder named have geven their wordes to stande thereunto and to fulfill the the same. That is to say—

Mr. William Chapell	John Periam
Simon Knight	John Davye
Thomas Bruarton	John Samforde
William Tryvet	Thomas Chapell
Nicholas Martyn	Nicholas Spicer
George Periam	Thomas Spicer
Thomas Martyn	Richard Swete
William Martyn	John Chapell
John Hutchyns	John Hackewell
Philipp Yarde	John Aplyn
John Levermore	Richard Dorchester."

Appendix

Although Mr. Stubbes appears to have been vested with the privileges of the port of Topsham, the Earl of Bedford must have had some share in them, as the following minute shows, and it also indicates that the annuity of £30 to Trewe and the other responsibilities attending the new watercourse were transferred from the chamber to the company.

"11 Nov. 1580. Memorandum that certen commytties hereafter are appointed to have conference together and to bring in a note to the Maior on Monday next, how the some of xx^{tie} markes shalbe collected and paied yerelie to the Right Honorable the Earle of Bedforde for the cranedge at Topsham : and also for xxx^{li} yerelie to be paied to one Trewe : and other rentes yerelie to be paid for the watercourse—

    Mr. John Hutchyns, Governor
    Mr. Nicholas Martyn
    Mr. Thomas Martyn
    Mr. John Davye
    Mr. Philipp Yarde
    Mr. William Martyn
    Mr. John Levermore
    Mr. Nicholas Spicer
    Mr. John Samforde."

"Mem. That the xix^{th} daye of November, 1580, the Companye being assembled ther was a bill reade : noted and drawen ouet by the commytties before named as rates upon certen merchandizes : for the saide some of xx^{tie} markes to be collected and paid yerelic to the saide Earle of Bedforde for the cranydge at Topsham, and other rente before resited, the coppie of which bill doo hereafter followe, viz."—(Not recorded).

"11 Jan. 1582. Whereas at this Courte John Watkyns hath brought in a bill of complaynt against the right Wor. Mr. Thomas Martyn, Maio', John Peryam, William Martyn, Jo

THE WEST GATE (EXTERIOR).

THE SOUTH GATE (EXTERIOR).

Appendix Samforde, Nicholas Spicer, and John Napers *alias* Sandye, for certen money due to hym by the saide parties, ffor hys travell and charges defrayed aboute the newe worke or watercourse of the Citie of Exeter, which he cannot receave of them. Wherefore hee prayeth to have lycence of this courte to recover the same by order of lawe. Therefore the Governo', with the consent and agreement of the generallitie, hath geven hym leave to commence lawe and procede therein against the saide parties and everie of theim for recoverie thereof."

The following extract from the Municipal Records shows in what manner the port was relieved of vexatious exactions, and completes the subject :—

"6 Nov. 1583. William Stubbes of Ratclyffe, Middlesex, to the Mayor, Bayliffs, and Commonalty of Exeter, Bond in £400, to secure a conveyance to the Mayor, Bayliffs, and Commonalty of 'all that the crane or key and cranage and sellers of the porte of Topsham with the appurtenances in the Countye of Devon, and the fyshinge in the water of Clyste in the sayd countye, together with all storehouses, sellers, sollers, roydet ground, and lande, and also all fees, offices, tolls, customes, pryvyledges, prehemynences, lyberties, profytts, and emoluments whatsoever to the said crane, key, and cranage, sellers, and fyshynge, or to anye of them in any wise belonginge, appertaynynge or incident,' for the term of thirty years, granted to him by letters patent, 16th May, 25 Elizabeth.

"Signed, W.. STUBBES."

The conveyance in similar terms follows.

As a walled and fortified city Exeter was probably better able to protect itself against external enemies during the earlier years of Elizabeth's reign than at any other period prior or past. If we may judge from the successful resistance to the protracted

Appendix siege of 1549, the walls, towers, bastions, and gates must have been in excellent order.

There was the Castle of Rougemont, almost impregnable in the strength of its position and defences: the approach from the city was by the great tower at the end of Castle street, which still remains a magnificent specimen of Norman architecture; the imposing arch, now within the grounds of the residence of Mrs. Gard, must have gained still greater impressiveness from the deep fosse at its base winding away on either side. The steeply scarped ground up to the wall is now laid out in tasteful walks which lead to a look-out tower. A modern structure has almost entirely displaced the original, but sufficient remains to indicate its position and utility. Commanding an extensive view of the surrounding country, it was a convenient spot from which to direct sorties of the garrison by the subterranean way and sallyport close adjacent.

Two bastions still remain in tolerable preservation, one in the grounds of the Club house commanding the approach from the north, and the other in the grounds of "The Vineyard," commanding the south and east. The city wall from Northernhay to the east end of Southernhay is no longer traceable except by a fragment which appears behind the premises of No. 266, High street. These premises were built of the materials taken from the eastgate which was removed in 1784, and the statue of Henry the Seventh which surmounted the exterior of the gate, now finds a place in a niche in the front of the modern building. At the back of the houses in Southernhay[1] the wall is still in tolerable preservation, and at the lower end, in the grounds of the Bishop's Palace, are the remains of the Barbican through which Bishop Carey, by an order of the Privy Council, obtained,

---

[1] The level of the gardens behind these houses is about 12ft. below that of the road in front. The fosse must have been of great depth, if we may judge from the made ground disclosed when the main drain was laid down.

ENTRANCE GATEWAY TO THE CASTLE.

THE GUILD HALL.

STATUE OF HENRY VII.

No 266, High Street, formerly on the Exterior Front
of the East Gate.

ST. PETER.

Corner of North Street.

Appendix in spite of the opposition of the Mayor and Corporation, an access to the open country in order to get the benefit of the air. The passage and wickets are still available, but are not now made use of.[1] A few yards further down are the remains of another tower, and adjoining are four embrasures the only ones to be found in the broken circuit of the walls. From this spot, down to the Water gate, the wall may be plainly traced. The gate is gone, and the battery tower, protecting it and the approaches from the river, is gone; but the arch in the wall behind the Custom house, still known as "Battery steps," indicates either a sallyport, or what is more probable, a means of access to the leat for the purpose of obtaining supplies of water. Proceeding further, we follow the course of the wall to West gate, the site of which is easily recognizable, but beyond this it extends but a few yards, when a considerable breach intervenes till we reach Bartholomew yard. At the corner, now occupied by Paradise place, stood Snayle Tower one of the principal western look-outs. The wall affords a terrace walk, between the two cemeteries, from this to Bartholomew-street, where we see that the houses on the left have their foundation on the wall itself, which is plainly discernible at the rear as seen from the yard of the "Crown and Sceptre" Inn. Crossing the road, over the site of the old North gate, and proceeding up Northernhay street, we have the wall on our right, and in one spot, just below the stonemason's yard, we trace faint indications of loopholes for the discharge of arrows. When the building of the Albert Memorial Museum necessitated the taking down of a portion of the city wall, a section of it revealed a beautiful specimen of herring-bone work,[2] a drawing of which was taken by Mr.

[1] The Bishop was required to build the bridge across the ditch on posts so that there should be no impediment to the flow of the water.

[2] The existence of this work, which was pointed out by Col. Harding to a party of the Archæological Society visiting Exeter 1861, is evidence of the antiquity of the wall as it now stands.

K

Appendix G. Townsend, and is now in his possession. With the continuation of the wall to the castle we have completed the circuit.³

The order of proceedings on election days will be best presented to the reader by extracting, verbatim, a copy of the minutes of one of those occasions. The day selected has no extraordinary features, but is a fair example of the business transacted at these annual meetings.

Sexto die Augusti 1597.

"The generall courte of thellecion of a newe Governor, Consulls, and other officers kepte and holden the vjth day of August 1597, and in the nyne and thirthieth yeare of the raigne of our Soveraigne ladie Elizabeth and accordinge to her Maties letters pattente.

Mr. Richard Dorchester, Governor.

Mr. Michaell Germyn,
Mr. William Martin, } Consulls.
John Tailor,

Mr. John Hackwill, Treasorer.

"In thellecion to be Governo' for this yeare followinge, viz.:
  Mr. Nicholas Martyn
  Mr. Christopher Spicer
  Mr. William Spicer

All which have chosen to be Governo' for this yeare followinge, viz.:
  Mr. Christopher Spicer,
            Governo', Jur.

---

³ Not many years since it was the custom for the Mayor and Corporation once in every year to perambulate the City walls—"beating the bounds" as it was termed. Due notice was given for all obstructions to be removed, and party-gates to be opened, so that the worshipful body might have free passage. What, with encroachment in some places, and destruction in others, but little of the wall is left to walk upon, and thanks to the energy of so-called modern improvers, at no distant period all trace of our historic monuments of the past will have been swept away.

Nos. 78 and 79 Fore Street.

Appendix "In thellecion to be Consulls for this yeare followinge, viz.:
    Mr. John Blackall
    Mr. George Smith
    Mr. Nicholas Martin
    Mr. John Davy
        Thomas Blackall
        Thomas Pope
    Mr. John Prouse
        Samuell Alford

And they have chosen to be Consulls for this yeare followinge, these fower persons hereunder named:
    Mr. Nicholas Martin,
    Mr. John Davye,
        Thomas Blackall, } Consulls.
        Thomas Pope,

"In the thellecion to be. Tresorer for this yeare followinge, viz.:
    Mr. John Ellacott
    Mr. Thomas Edwardes
        Jasper Horsey

And they have chosen for there Tresorer, viz.:
    Mr. John Ellacott, Tresorer, Jur.

"Auditors assigned to take the olde Tresorers accompte.

At this Courte it is ordered that Mr. John Ellacott, Tresorer this yeare, Jasper Horsey and Walter Burrowe shalbe Auditors to take and peruse the accompte of Mr. John Hackwill, Treasorer, the last yeare to be ended at or on thisside the next Courte, and to certifie the same at the saide Courte, and that they shall sett downe what the clarke shall have for writtinge extraordinarie this yeare.

"Goodes delivered by the olde Governo' to the new Governo'

Also at this Courte Mr. Richarde Dorchester oure late Governo' delivered in open Courte to Mr. Christopher Spicer our newe Governo' the Charter of the Companie, the letters of armes belonginge to the same, an Anuytie of Mr. Prestwoodes, the seale belonginge to this Companie and Mrs. Tuckfeildes kaic.

Appendix "John Mallott took the othe of a ffreeman as an apprentice within his terme. } Also at this Courte John Mallott the apprentice of Ignacius Jurden took the othe of a ffreeman as an apprentice within his terme, and was sworn Jur., and paide the ffees of the Courte, viz.: vs—Md. That xii$d$ was delivered Mr. Tresorer for the box and vj$d$ for absence of Mr. William Martin, Jun', Consull.

"Likewise at this present Courte there was a draught for an Acte reade, that everie ffreeman of this Companie that doth owe anie ffine or amercyament to this Companie the same being demanded and not paide within three daies and written into the Blacke booke, to paie dubble, wch acte is referred over untill some other conveynient time.

"xxi$s$ given to the S'iants of Lyme. } Also at this Courte there was a colleccon made for this Companie for William Welch one of the Seriants at Macc in Lyme, which did amounte to xix$s$, and for as much as the saide poore man's daughter did marrie with Arthur Jurden a ffreeman of this Companie deceassed, who hath left three children behind him, the saide Welch takinge uppon him to discharge the Cittie of the keping and bringinge uppe of the saide children, it was therefore thought good by the whole Companie that the saide some of xix$s$ shalbe made full xl$s$, and that Mr. Tresorer shall disburse towards the payment thereof xxj$s$.

xij$d$ paid Mr. Tresorer. ... Md. That William Horsham and Peter Sampson paid ech of them xii$d$ for not wearinge there gowndes at thelleccon daie, accordinge to a certeine act hertofore made, uppon whose submission they had given them backe againe vj$d$ a peece and so paide the Tresorer xij$d$."

GOVERNORS OF THE GUILD.   57

Appendix "iiij*s* paid by Mr. William Spicer for John Chappell to oure Tresorer. Also at this Courte Mr. William Spicer paide for John Chappell, Jun'. to Mr. Tresorer for his quarterledge dewe the last yeare iiij*s*.

"Twentie markes to be pd by John Morrys for the averidge this yeare. At this Courte it is agreed by the Governor, Consulls, and whole Companie that John Morrys shall have the averidge for this yeare followinge, that is to saie, from the vjth of August 1597, untill the vjth of August 1598, for twentie markes, and hath putt in sureties for answeringe thereof, Mr. William Spicer and David Bagwill, who took uppon them to seale to this Companie at the next Courte with the said John Morrys ech of them a bill for payment of vj*l* xiij*s* iiij*d* at the end of the said yeare.

"v*l* paid by Alexander Germyn and Robert Parr for William Tucker. Also at this Courte Alexander Germyn and Robert Parr paid Mr. John Hackwill, Tresorer, v*l*, viz.: either of them 1*s*, wch they gave there wordes and promis to this Companie for the broake of William Tucker, and praied that the same might be entered uppon the boocke to thende they might have recovery against the said Tucker.

"Fforasmuch as these persons hereunder named did absent themselves at thelleccon daie, therefore they and evry of them shall paie accordinge to a certeine Act:
        George Drake,
        Phillippe Yeard,
        Oliver Tapper."

XV. The concluding—to some the most important—business of the day is the Governor's dinner, towards the expense of which he is allowed the sum of five marks, and if he "doo provide a bucke to the said dynner he shall have allowed him also xiijs iiijd for the same over and above his other allowance." He is also paid "five shillings to be bestowed towardes the pot to be boyled for the poore prisoners in the Queene's gayell."

There are some amusing perplexities in respect of these Governors' dinners. It was no doubt a sacred point with the members that they should, first, take place; and, secondly, if possible, on the 6th day of August, the memorable anniversary of the raising of the siege of Exeter. Now Friday was a fish day, and Saturday was not a flesh day, and Sunday was not to be thought of; and at certain recurring periods it naturally happened that the 6th of August would fall on one of those days. To fix a day to suit everybody's convenience and be agreeable to the Governor was a problem not easily solved.

In 1599 Mr. Martin the Governor was singularly afflicted. He happened to be Mayor at the same time, and it was the custom of the Mayor (as confirmed by the minute I consult) to entertain on Mondays. The election day happened to fall on a Monday, and the Merchant's Hall not being large enough to contain so many guests, or it being contrary to etiquette to entertain those not free of the Company therein, it was decided that the double banquet should be served in his own house.

During the famine in 1596, the Court began to discuss the dinner question a month before the day the feast became due, and charitably decided that there should be "no dynner kept and that the money allowed for that purpose shoulde be imployed in corne and geven to poore householders;" but, alas, for the weakness of all human resolves! Not a week had elapsed ere the Court resolved that they could not give up the dinner, but the poor should be fed all the same, and 8*l* 8*s* 6*d* was voted for that purpose.

But the real business of the Courte is transacted at the ordinary meetings.

RED LION COURT, MAGDALENE STREET.

Appendix

We are introduced to a somewhat disagreeable phase of the social life of the period by frequent references to contentions and quarrels. Religious differences would, of course, be a fertile source of acrimonious argumentation; but the growing freedom of thought and action, and a commerce expanding under the genial influence of State encouragement (engendering keen competition and rivalry), would naturally lead to opinions too plainly outspoken, and disputes too warmly contested. A very strong regulation was established in 1572 against "brawlinge and ffyghtinge," which it seems had previously prevailed, and any witness of such unseemly conduct was required to present the same to the Court under a penalty of fine. Notwithstanding, we find that at the Court held 24th February, 1575, it was certified, "That not onlie John Levermore spake unseemelie and opprobrous wordes to Richarde Swete, but also that Richarde Swete spake the like wordes unto the saide John Levermore: Therefore it is agreed that ether of them shall paye his broke to the howse, accordinge to an acte heretofore made in that behalf, which is iijs iiijd a pece: And for that also there was unseemelie and uncourtuose wordes spoken at this Courte betwene George Periman and Thomas Martyn in the presence of the Governo' Consultes and whole Companye, therefore it is also agreed upon by the saide Governo', &c., that ether of theim shall paye to this Companye for their defaulcte therein iijs iiijd."

XX.

At the same Court "Richarde Denys was presented for nastic and opprobrous wordes wch hee gave of late to Richarde Purye, being a freeman of Companye, at the Busshops Palace."

In the following year John Davye the Treasurer was presented "for unseemelie wordes, wh hee gave of late to Davy Vilvaine in Northinghay: wherefore it is adiudged by the whole Companye the said John Davye shall pay to this societie iijs iiijd, so upon his submission and payment thereof the Governo' gave hym backe ageyne xvjd."

Appendix   In June 1576, it was "enacted, ordeyned, and throughelie agreed upon, That whatsoever hee be, beinge free of this Companye, that doeth hereafter speake any slaunderous, unsemelie, or unhonest wordes, by any other his bretheren free of this Companye whether they be in presence, or beinge absent, that everie suche pson shall paye to this societie, for suche his ill behaviour, suche greate ffyne as shalbe thought good by the Governo', &c."

In June 1593, "it is presented that Willm. Chappell did assaulte and stricke John Dipforde" and was fined xvj*s* viij*d*. In September following "Jasper Horsey doth present Pawle Trigge for speakinge of unsemely wordes by hime," for which he had to pay iij*s* iiij*d*, reduced to 1*s* on his submission.

XXI. In July in the following year John Hackwill discovered that Clement Owleborrowe and his son had been guilty of adventuring, not being free of the Company, and was subject to "unsemelie wordes" from the delinquent, who was presented for both offences.

XXII. From the minutes we find the Clerk, John Felde, was appointed at a salary of 13*s* 4*d* a year—payable quarterly—with perquisites for preparing charter parties and indentures of apprentices. That "a new ansine of redd and grene sylke sarcenet" was purchased for £4 10*s* 3*d*. That Mr. Doctor Tremayne interceded for Robert Prowse, and got his fine for a "broke" mitigated. That Morice Downe is to have the stock of the house, £20 (on loan), in consideration of great loss at sea by rovers. That apprentices trading on their own account shall pay 6*s* 8*d* to the house, 6*d* to the Clerk, and 4*d* to the "Bedell." That woman's rights were admitted when Widow Webber was lent the £20 house money.

That an apprentice of a freeman was bound to claim the freedom of the Company within a year, under the penalty of £10, and was also required to be free of the City. That every

THE NORTH GATE (EXTERIOR).

Appendix son instead of the eldest only) of every freeman may be admitted.

XXIII. That 13s 4d annually was left by the will of John Ellacott for a "belman that goeth by night."

XXIV. That William Prouse was admitted a freeman at the request of Sir William Periam, Lord Chief Baron of the Exchequer, and John Prouse at the solicitation of the Earl of Essex, and that the said John was subsequently fined for using "unseemlie" words on Northernhay.

XXV. That there is much discussion on the reformation of kersaies and woollen goods, and we are suddenly startled by an order that James Boyer for "comittinge of a murder uppon one hay-
XXVI. man ys by the handes of the whole Companie dismissed."

We acquire also some information as to the value of musical instruments in the memo. that "Mr. Yarde hath bought a new drome at London which cost xlvij*s* iiij*d* and hath solde o' olde drome for xx*s*."

One minute discloses a curious mode of settling a difficulty :—
"1st July 1589. At this Courte ther was certaine controversie betwene the howse and Mr. John Blackall, concerninge certaine money by him demanded of the saide howse, which said controversie was before this tyme referred to the order and determinacon of Mr. Thomas Chappell, Maio', and Mr. John Peryam, which said controversie ys nowe by them determined. And they do awarde that the said John Blackall shalbe paied by the Treasorer of this Companie of tenne shillings in money and syxe shillinges towardes the buying of a velvett night cappe. And so the said John Blackall doth acquitt the whole Companie of all manner of matters from the beginninge of the wourlde untill this presente daie."

Let us not be irreverent on the subject of night caps. Dr. Doran tells us that in the days of Elizabeth and James no Puritan divine ever went to bed but with his head in a night cap

L.

Appendix¹ of black silk tipped with white, and doctors of medicine and privy councillors sank to rest in night caps wrought with gold silk. It might have been with these worthies, as it was with the lady of story, that they wished to present a creditable appearance in case of fire; and really the contingency of a sudden exposure to the gaze of the profane was a very probable one. In the inventory of the goods and chattels of the Guild will be found, amongst other things, twenty-four leather buckets and an iron crook. This latter instrument was for the purpose of pulling down the gables and woodwork of the houses adjoining one that XXVII. happened to be on fire, in order to prevent its spreading.

The principal trade being with France a lively interest would of course be taken by the merchants in the French import duties.

In 1572 there appears to have been a commercial treaty entered into with the French King, which is alluded to in the following correspondence:—

"21st August 1572. Also at this Courte there was a lre delivered to the Governor, Consulls, and Companye, directed to them and others the Marchauntes of Tottnesse, by certen Commissioners at London, the copie whereof foloweth—

"in dorso. To o' very lovinge ffriendes John Peter, William Chapell, George Peryman, Thomas Martyn, Richarde Swete, John Davye of Exeter, Richarde Enery, Walter Dowse, John Wise, Luke Serrel, Gefferey Babb, Nicholas Balle of Totnesse and other of theim, and to all other the westren marchauntes occupyinge Ffraunce or thereabouts. After o' hartie commendacions, whereas wee and others have to consider of the trade nowe in ffraunce to be stablyshed by the late league made between the Q. matie and the ffrenche Kynge: And that yee have understandinge and good knowledge of the newe exactions and other thinges eneros to o' Marchauntes that are taken upon theim o' late, sethens the begynninge of her highnes reigne, in

Appendix. Morles, S. Mallowes, Vitrie, and other places in Britayne or ellswhere thereaboute, where your western Marchauntes doo trade, and what dewe customes ought to be paid both for oure owne and forryn commodities there : Wee require and will youe on her Maties. behalf, that youe and other the skylfullest in this trade repaier and consider together thereupon, and that two of the sufficientest of youe in skyll and knowledge thereof repayer unto us furthwith hether to London, to set downe the same in wrytinge, that wee maye consider upon the same, and howe it maye be ordered best for youre proffit and the whole subjectes of the realme. Wherefore we praye youe not to fayle, as you will answere upon youre perryll. ffar you well, from London the ixth of August 1572.

Yo' loving friends
Thomas Mylton,
Valentine Dalye,
Pet. Erborne."

"in dorso   To the worshipfull Mr. Richarde Every, Maior of Totnesse, Mr. Walter Dowse and other the Marchauntes of the saide towne of Totnesse geave thes :—

Whereas this present xxvth of August wee have receaved a lre from certen Commissioners at London, directed as well to youe as unto us, touchinge matters, to be answered theim furthwith as yee shall perceave by the said lre, which wee sende unto youe by this bearer, which letter wee desire youe to send us ageyne, and to call the Marchauntes of youre towne together, and to take some order to answere the same, and to appoint one most meetest to ryde to London for that purpose and wee will appointe an other.   And yf it please any of youe to come to Exon, to confer with us as touchinge the effect of the saide lre, wee wilbe glad to commen with youe therein : So as youe and

L²

Appendix wee may agree together and make oure answere accordinglie: Wee doo determyne that he whome wee will sende shalbe readie by the ende of this weeke at the ffurthest. And thus fare yee hartelie well. ffrom Exon the xxv of August, 1572.

By youres to commande T. Prestwood, Governo' of the Companye of Marchauntes Adventurers of Exon."

"25 August 1572. At which Courte the Governo', Consulls, and Companye have appointed those parsons of the Companye whose names are hereinunder wryten, to conferr and geve theim to understande as touchinge the newe customes in ffraunce, according to a lre directed to theim from certen Commissioners at London, That is to saye:—

    John Dare
    Philipp Yarde
    Richard Swete
    John Barstable
    Thomas Chapell
    John Chapell
    William Paramore
    John Shere

"Also at this Courte there came in and dyd appere from Totnesse (upon a lre sente unto theim) three of the Marchauntes of their Towne to conferr with o' companye, as touchinge the effect of the saide lre, namelie:—

    Mr. John Wyse
    Gefferey Babb
    Nicholas Ball

Which letter was as well directed to the saide Marchauntes of Totnesse and other the Marchauntes there as unto us."

"Wheareas at a Courte holden the xxvth of this psent moneth of August 1572, the Governor, Consulls, and Company, did

THE EAST GATE (EXTERIOR).

Appendix receave a lre from certen Commissioners at London, for matters to be aunswered unto theim furthwith. Therefore the saide Governo', Consulls, and Companye, accordinge to the teano' of the saide lre have appointed one of this Companye to ride to London to aunswere the same."

"And farther the saide Governo', Consulls, and Companye have agreed at the saide Courte that those of the saide Companye whose names are hereunder wryten shall bere and pay towards the charges thereof as they are hereafter rated, that is to saye :"—

[Sixty-two members were rated in sums of from half-a-crown to sixpence towardes these charges, and £3 8s 6d was the sum total.]

"The coppie of a lre sent by this Companye to the Commissioners at London as answere unto their letter.

"Right Worshipfulls o' humble commendacions yee shall understande that wee have receaved yor lre bearinge date the ixth daye of this present moneth of August which came not unto o' handes, untill the xxvth of the saide moneth : But assone as we receaved the same and had perused it, dyd sende the saide lre to Totnesse to the Marchauntes there being as well directed unto theim as unto us : And furthwith caused the Marchauntes of Exon to come together, who did conferr as touchinge the effect of your saide lre : And thereuppon dyd appointe one of the Marchauntes of or towne of Exon, namelie Richard Swete, and the Marchauntes of Totnesse have appointed an other, the skylfullest amonge us in knowledge, as touchinge the newe customes in ffraunce, who will repaier unto yor worshippes, and geve youe to understande thereof, desiringe you to accept theim in oure behalf. And thus wee commyt youre worshippes to the tuicion of Almightie God who alwaies preserve you : from Exon the xxxth of August 1572."

This difficulty appears to have been satisfactorily surmounted, for no further complaint is recorded for nearly ten years. In

Appendix 1582, however, new troubles are heralded by an order from the Lord Treasurer of England, " to restrain all shipping that meanes to goo for Burdeaux, Nante, and other places of Fraunce."

In the following year the storm bursts. The Merchants determined to leave no means untried to relieve themselves from the oppressive exactions of the French customs, entered upon a suit, which, extending over two years and entailing much trouble and expense, was, it may be inferred, carried to a successful issue. Indicative of the times is the "douceur" to the French Ambassador on the conclusion of the dispute. The minutes relating to this suit are all here entered in their proper order.

"4 Sept. 1582. At this Courte ther was the copie of a lre reade from the Right Honorable the L. Threasorer of Englande, directed to the customer and other officers of her Maties porte of Exon, restrayning all shipping that meanes to goo for Burdeaux, Nante, and other places of ffraunce to lade wynes, not to departe before the   daye of   next ensuing: which lre beres date the   of   1582."

"15 April 1583. The names of the strangers of the Townes adjoining that were presente at this Courte. (They were summoned to confer with the Company respecting a new customs duty).

Mr. Voysey
William Blackaller } of Totnes
Richard Blackaller

Edwarde Amye ...of Tyverton

Mr. Robert Henley
Thomas Ffisher } of Taunton

Mr. Phillibert Selwood
Harry Samwayes } of Charde

Philipp Cockeram
James Skynner } of Collomton

"At this Courte it is agreed that everie Marchaunte free of this Companye which doo trade into the parties of Britayne shall certifie their factors that lyeth in the saide parties that they doo not paye any money for this newe custome latelie raysed in

Appendix Britayne, but that they paye it by protest untill they knowe whether it be a dutie to be paied or not : until farder order be taken therein. And if any charges as well heretofore past as also hereafter to be laied oute touching the suyte thereof, those parsons that doeth appere at this Courte of the Townes adjoining doo promise to procure the Marchauntes of their townes ·that be traders thether that they shalbe contributory to the same accordinge to their porcions of adventuring as Exeter doeth : and bring their handes to a bill for the same by the xxvth daie of this instante moneth of Aprill : In witness whereof they have subscribed their names."

The Courte kept and holden the 11th June, 1583, and continued open until the 14th following inclusive.

Merchants of other towns summoned :—

Mr. John Levermore, Governo'
Mr. John Blackaller } Consulls
Twosse

Mr. Thomas Pope thelder } Taunton
John Pope, the youner

Mr. Christopher Saverye
Mr. Nicholas Ball
Mr. Luke Tryvet
Mr. Harry Everye } of Totnes
Mr. Nicholas Newman
Nicholas Hayman
William Ducke

Mr. Phillibert Selwood } of Charde
Harry Samwayes
Edward Amye ...of Tiverton

" At. this Courte ther was a lre reade from the right wo' Sir Ames Poulet and Sir Thomas Leighton Knt., her Maties Governors of the Isles of Jersey and Garnesey, as touchinge ther frendeshippes and furtheraunce for an incorporacion to be had for the trade of Brytayne, to be reduced into the saide islandes (which lre was also published and reade at the last Courte) for which cause the Companye beinge assembled with dyverse Marchauntes of other townes adioyning, and had moche debatinge touchinge the same, and at last for dyverse causes beinge alleged dyd finde it verie inconvenient for the estate of the commonwealth that in the tyme of peace the saide trade shoulde be brought into the saide llandes : Whereupon it was ordered that lres shouldē be wreten to the saide S. Ames Poulet and Sir Thomas Leighton to this effecte : viz., to geve them thanckes for their goode will in that behalf : And also to praye theim to stande oure good frendes in oure suyte, which wee pretende to presente for the suppressinge the newe customes and exactions lately raysed upon us in the parties of ffraunce and Britayne.

" And for the presentinge of the saide suyte the companye dyd then consider that it was requisite to have some fit and skylfull man that woulde take the paynes to preferr and folowe the saide suyte as well to the Queenes hignes and her moste honorable Counsell : as also unto the Ffrenche kinge, Whereupon there was nominated two parsons which the Companye thought most fitteste for that purpose : viz., Andrewe Geare of Exeter, and Thomas Pope the younger of Taunton. So it was put to be judged by handes, so the Companye dyd chuse and appointe the saide Thomas Pope to be their Attorney and Deputie in this behalf.

" Also the Companye had then to consider howe the saide Thomas Pope shoulde be answered and paied for his paynes and charges that he shoulde be at about the presentinge of the saide suyte, and at last dyd conclude and agree : That if the saide Thomas Pope doo obteyne the saide suyte and get us free of the saide newe customes then he is to have for his paynes over and besides his reasonable charges and expences two hundred crownes : And if he cannot obteyne the same then he is to have over and besides his saide charges and expences but one hundred crownes towards his paynes. Provided alwayes that if the saide Thomas Pope goo no farther then London and cannot obteyne his suyte ther, then hee is to be ordered for his travell and paynes besides his reasonable charges and expences as the Marchauntes of Exon and other the townes and places aforesaide shall thinke good.

" And also it is ordered at this Courte that a suplication shalbe wreten from us unto the right honorable Lord-therle of Bedforde to let hym to understande of our suyte before wee proceede

Appendix. therein, and to request his hono' with the rest of the Ll. and others of her Maties most honorable Privie Counsell, to direct ther favorable lres unto her Maties Imbassadors in Ffraunce for the redresse thereof. And farther it is thought good that the saide Thomas Pope shall have a lre of Attorney from us to authorize hym to deale for us in oure saide suyte."

"13 June. Ther was a suplication which was appointed at oure laste Courte to be sente from us unto the right honorable Lorde therle of Bedforde for his furtheraunce of oure suyte which wee pretende for the suppressinge of the newe customes latelie raysed upon Marchauntes in the parties of Ffraunce and Brytayne.

"Also ther was made a Lre of Attorney made by the Companye and the Marchauntes of other townes adjoyning: To Thomas Pope of Taunton, Marchaunte, authorizing hym to presente oure saide suyte.

"Also ther was reade a bill in what order the charges and paynes of the saide Thomas Pope shalbe paied and answered unto hym: which hee shalbe at and layed oute aboute the saide suyte. All which lres and writinges beinge reade were subscribed aswell by the handes of dyverse Marchauntes of Exeter, as also by sundry other Marchauntes of Totnes, Tyverton, and Collompton:· And forasmoche as ther wanted the handes of those of Taunton, Charde, and Lyme, the Companye dyd order that the saide lres and writinges should be sente to the saide Thomas Pope at Taunton that hee may repayer unto theim to get ther handes thereunto as hee had promised.

"Also it was ordered at this Courte: That a bill of instructions shouldbe made and sente also from us unto the saide Thomas Pope with the saide lres and writinges for his better instruction therein: the coppie of which bill of instructions doo hereafter ensue, viz.:—

"14 June 1583. Lres and instructions to be delivered and geven to our trustie frende Thomas Pope the younger of Taunton Marchaunte, as touchinge oure suyte which wee commyte unto hym for the suppressinge of the newe customes and exactions latelye raysed upon Inglishe Marchauntes in the parties of Ffraunce and Brytayne.

"Ffirst youe shall receave two lres to the right Wo' Sir Ames Poulet and S' Thomas Leighton Knights, her Maties Governo' of the Isles of Jersey and Garnsey, as answere unto their Wo' lre.

"Also a supplication from us to the right honorable Lorde therle of Bedforde.

"Also oure Lre of Attorney whereby wee authorize youe to presente oure suyte.

"Also oure bill for the aunswereinge of youe for youre paynes and charges to be taken therein.

"All which lres and writings wee praye youe accordinge to youre promise to get some of the anciente Marchauntes of the townes of Taunton, Charde, and Lyme, to subscribe thereunto as wee of Exeter, Totnes, Tyverton, and Collompton have done.

"Ite oure mynde is: That youe sende us the bills from Taunton, Charde, and Lyme subscribed with the handes of suche as wilbe contributory to the charges of this oure saide suyte accordinge to their promisses as well of Exeter and other places have done, before you proceede or goo any farther in our saide suyte.

"Also oure mynde is: That if you have no good lykinge that oure saide suyte will take place when youe be at London, that youe staye the presentinge thereof and proceede no farther therein.

"And wee praye youe, that if you goo thro with this oure suyte: That with as moche conveniente speede as youe maye, youe sende us worde from tyme to tyme aswell when youe are at London as beyonde the seas howe all thinges doo passe, that you may have answere from us with the best ayde wee can for your furtheraunce therein.

"And it is ordered at this Courte: That where' Mr. Levermore oure Governo' on the behalf of the Companye and at their request hath put his hande to the bill for the answereinge of Thomas Pope for his charges and paynes to be taken aboute oure saide suyte, the whole Companye doo promise and agree to see hym acquitted and discharged thereof, as the averedges shall arise.

"And further it is agreed and ordered that Mr. Thomas Spicer and Richarde Swete shall collecte and gather upp all suche averedges of this porte of Exeter, as is latelie appointed for to be collected, towardes the defraying of the charges for the sup-

THE FRENCH SUIT. 71

Appendix. pressing of the newe customes lately raysed in the parties of Ffraunce and Brytayne: And they to be allowed reasonablie for their paynes."

"Memorandum that the xiiijth daye of June 1583, ,oure Governo' did receave from the Marchauntes of Totnes a lre being directed from Mr. Thomas Wylson, Valentine Dalye, and Peter Edborough, Commyssioners, dated ixth of August in anno 1572, directed as well to the Marchauntes of Exeter as those of Totnes, touchinge certene newe customes then raysed in dyverse places in the parties of Brytayne, onnerous to oure Inglishe Marchauntes. And therewithall dyd receave from those of Totnes a bill of Customes at Morles, before the Queene's Maties reigne in anno 1588.

"And also dyd receave an other bill of customes at Saint Malowes, in her Maties reigne in anno 1572. And also an other bill conteyning the custome due at Roan upon cloth in anno 1558.

"Which lre and bills of customes oure saide Governo' dyd sende furthwith unto the saide Thomas Pope that hee maye shewe theim unto his Counsell whereby it might be a furtheraunce of his suyte."

"16 Oct. 1583. At this Courte Robert Pope of Taunton brought in a bill of exchaunge of xviij$l$ iij$s$ ix$d$ made by Thomas Pope the younger of Taunton, oure Attorney for the presenting oure suyte for the suppressing of the newe customes latelie raysed upon Inglishe Marchauntes in the parties of Ffraunce and Brytayne. But bycause the saide bill was directed to one Richard Skynner of London and not unto this Companye, nor had any certificate from the saide Thomas Pope touching the some: Yt was referred untill this Companye have further understanding thereof."

" 3 Dec. 1583. At this Courte Thomas Pope the younger of Taunton, oure Attorney for the obteyning of oure suyte at the Courte of Ffraunce is latelie retorned from thence, came in and declared of his proceedinges therein, and gave us to understande that hee had not as yet gone through with the saide suyte but had good hope the same maye be obteyned very shortly if it be folowed. And brought in an order or decree from the saide Courte of Ffraunce touching the same under the right honorable

S' Henry Cobham, Knight, Lorde Imbassadour there. And also brought in his accompt of expences and charges which hee hath byn at in the prosecuting of the saide suyt : Whereupon it is ordered at this Courte that the saide Thomas Pope shall have paied hym upon a reckning lx$l$, and that the Marchauntes of Totnes, Lyme, and Exeter, shall disburse and paye furthwith xx$l$ oute of everie place, untill suche tyme as the Marchauntes of those places and of thother townes adioyning maye come together and bring in the accompte of everie place and the money collected towardes the defraying of the saide charge that everie place maye bere his parte indifferentlie."

"6 August 1584. It is ordered that Mr. John Davie o' newe Governo' this yeare, Mr. John Sampforde and Richard Bevis shalbe audito' to peruse and take the accompte of Thomas Pope for his travaile into Ffraunce about o' late suyte at the Courte ther, and for Mr. Sweetes accompte for money collected by him towardes the defrainge of the charge thereof, and also for o' clarkes accompte and what money he shall have for wrettinge of lres and makinge of other wrettinges and paines takinge theraboute, and bringe in there proceadinges at the next Courte."

"28 August 1584. It is ordered that Mr. Sweete shall ride to Totnes aboute the collection for the ffrench suite, and he to be reasonably considered for his paines and to have the Governo' lre.

"(same day). The Auditors appointed at the laste Courte for the auditinge and perusinge of Thomas Popes accompte as touchinge his travell and charges aboute the ffrench suite do finde dewe uppon his saide accompte and all charge aboute the same iiijxx vij$l$ which is for everye division a xxix$l$, viz. :

ffor Exeter xxix$l$
ffor Tottenes xxix$l$
ffor Lyme xxix$l$

"Also the said Auditors do finde that Mr. Sweete hath receaved clere of all charge a xxiiij$l$ iij$s$ jd, of which some is paid to the saide Thomas Pope a xx$l$, so there resteth unto hime by Exeter a vj$l$ xij$s$ xd, which xij$s$ xd the Auditors do appointe that John ffeilde o' clarke shall have it, because they thinke is to littell considered for his paines which is but a xlvij$s$ 11d, which hee is

Appendix. to be paied oute of the saide reste. Of which vj*l* xij*s* x*d* ther remaynes in Mr. Sweetes handes gathered the xviij August 1584, xxxvj*s*, besides John Ffeildes money which is xlvij*s* ij*d*. So there remaynes to Thomas Pope to be gathered by Exeter men a iiij*l* xvj*s* x*d*.

Towardes payment of which

Tottenes owes for fardells and packe cxxj	vj*l* xij*s*
Thomas Broderidge of Stanton owes for xxiij fardells and packes	xxiij*s*
Taunton owes for lxij fardells and packes	iij*l* ij*s*
Collompton owes for lxv fardells and packes	iij*l* v*s*
Tiverton owes for xxxij packes and fardells	xxxij*s*
Exeter owes for xxix packes and fardells	xxix*s*

Which accompte was audited the xviijth daie of August 1584, and brought in at this Courte."

"12 Nov. 1584. Thomas Popes' acquittance in respect of Exeter and Tottenes brought in."

"16 April 1585. At this Courte there was lre reade from the Ll. of her Maties moste honorable privie Counsell directed to Sir Robte. Dennys, S' John Gibble, Knights, Peter Edgecombe, and John ffits, Esquiers, dated the xvith daie of January 1584 (o.s.) touchinge sixe hundred ffrenche crownes to be paid to one Bickner of London (for a suite by hime followed in Roian for the suppressinge of newe customes lately raised there uppon Inglishe comodities) whereof iiij*c* crownes is to be levied of the Merchauntes of London tradinge to Roian, and the rest being ij*c* crownes is to be levied by the Merchauntes of the west parte tradinge thither : And the matter being moved by o' generalite they coulde not agree thereuppon. But for that Mr. Walter Buggins and Mr. Nicholas Gudridge of Totnes were appointed by the Councells lres to see the levienge of the said ij*c* crownes of the Merchauntes of the west parte, the matter was referred untill they did conferr with the Merchauntes of their towne of Tottenes to understande what order they will take therein, and then if it please the said Mr. Buggins and Mr. Goodridge to repaire hether on the Sessions week next to let the Companie to understande thereof, they will do therein that shalbe for theim reasonable.

Appendix. "And it is ordered that a lre shalbe written to the said Mr. Buggins and Mr. Goodridge to let them understande the Companies minde herein."

"15 April 1585. Also it is ordered at this Courte that o' Treasorer Mr. Sampforde shall paie unto Mr. Richard Prouse one of the Burgesses of this Parliament for the Cittie of Exeter the some of iij*l* iiij*s* which he hath laied oute at the said parliament tyme about the suyte of the Companie.

"And further it is ordered that o' Treasorer Mr. Sampforde shall procure those persones-hereafter named to be arrested and sued the lawe for certaine money which is not paied to warde the answeringe of Thomas Pope for his charge aboute the ffrenche suite, viz. :—

William Blackaller } of Totnes
Richard Blackaller }
Edward Amye ...of Tiverton
Phillipp Cocram ...of Cullompton

"And also the saide Mr. Sampforde is to gather uppe what became of the Merchauntes of Tiverton and the Merchauntes of Exeter which are behinde towardes the said payment.

"And it is further ordered and agreed that thoise that do disburse and lende anye money to the use aforesaid shalbe allowed after the rate of xij*d* the packe uppon suche wares as they sende to Roane, and all those that do not lende anie money to the said use shall paie ij*s* uppon every packe of suche wares as they send thither. And likewise all strangers that do lade within o' porte to paie ij*s* of every packe also that they sende thither (except those of Totnes and Lyme). And it is ordered that the said money be levied upon everie packe after the rate and order aforesaid untill the said some of xij*l* be collected. And then all thoise that have lent anie money to that aforesaid it shalbe repaied them againe by suche severall porcions as they have laied oute. And the saide John ffollett and Walter Borrough to collecte the same and geve accompte thereof."

"16 Dec. 1585. At this Courte there was a lre reade from Nicholas Samuell Alforde and Walter Harrison in Roane, as touchinge one thousand crownes to be lente unto the Right Honorable S' Edwarde Stafforde, Knight, Lorde Imbasador in

THE FRENCH SUIT.

Appendix. ffraunce, by the Merchauntes of London and the west, parte whereof is to be collected and lente by the Merchauntes of the west parte 200 crownes and the rest by those of London, of which 200 crownes the Merchauntes of Totnes are to lent 145 crownes, and 25 by those of Exeter, which lre was directed to o' Governor Mr. Thomas Chappell and the Consulls as a bill of exchange. But forasmuche as ther was litle apparences at this Courte the matter was referred untill the next Courte to be considered of."

"Memorandu that the first daie of June 1585, the Merchauntes of Exeter and Totnes being assembled in the Merchauntes haule in Exeter, do think this to be a reasonable porcion to be levied of everye towne hereafter mencioned as touchinge the two hundred ffrenche crownes to be answered to one Bickner of London by the Merchauntes of the west parte tradinge to Roane, viz.,:—

of Southampton	xx Crownes
of Poole	x Crownes
of Waymouth	xxx Crownes
of Lyme Rege	xx Crownes
of Exeter and Totnes	between them vi^{xx}Crownes"

"10 July 1585. Note that where order is taken that there shalbe levied of the Merchauntes of the Cittie of Exeter the some of xij*l* towardes the payment of Bickners money: Therefore at this Courte it is ordered and enacted by the Governor, Consulls, and Companie, that those persons whose names are hereunder subscribed shall disburse and lende towardes the payment thereof suche some of money as to everye of them is appointed, viz.:—

Mr. John Davie Maio'	xxx*s*	John Backwill	v*s*
Mr. Nicholas Martyn	xx*s*	Thomas Walker	xx*s*
Mr. Thomas Martyn	xx*s*	Richard Bevis	v*s*
Mr. Willm. Martyn	x*s*	Richard Dorchester	v*s*
Mr. John Levermore	v*s*	John ffollett	v*s*
Mr. Harry Ellacott	x*s*	Thomas Bridgeman	x*s*
Mr. Thomas Chappell	x*s*	Richard Jurden	x*s*
Mr. Nicholas Spicer	x*s*	Walter Borrough	x*s*

Appendix.

Mr. Thomas Spicer	xs	Walter Horssey	vs
Mr. John Chappell	xs	Jasper Horssey	vs
Mr. Richard Sweete	vs	Robert Sherwoode	xs
Mr. John Howell	xs		

"And it is also ordered that John Ffollett and Walter Borrough shall collecte the saide money of the saide parties."

XXVIII. Disputes and complaints with France were of constant occurrence, arising from the insecure state of the Channel, owing to pirates and rovers of the nations infesting the coasts. In 1586 Duke Mercurye's fine ship laden with wines was taken by the Bark "Burr" of London, and in retaliation he seized all the ships and their cargoes belonging to Exeter, which were then in the port of Morlaix. Our merchants offered to make ample restitution, and with the assistance of Lord Burghley, the dispute it is presumed was settled. We have the grievance however of exactions and oppressive duties occasionally cropping up until

XXIX. 1598, when one Medlande of Totnes proposes to smooth all difficulties for £300.

XXX. During all this time it was frequently under discussion to bring the trade to the isles of Jersey and Guernsey, so as to avoid the French coasts altogether, and lessen the risks from pirates on that side the channel.

XXXI. Touching these pirates, they appear to have been particularly troublesome about the year 1578, for we find that a Queen's ship was specially requested by the Merchants to be stationed off our coast for the protection of the shipping, and £100 was ordered to be collected towards defraying the expense. In answer to the request, however, Her Majesty most graciously showed her confidence in Exeter men, and voluntarily granted them a commission to fit out their own war ship with the same powers and privileges as the Queen's ships possessed. "Most humblie dutifullie and thankfullie" did the Merchants receive this royal

STAIRCASE IN "KING JOHN TAVERN,"
Formerly in South Street.

SPANISH DIFFICULTIES.

Appendix XXXII.
XXXIII.
mark of favour; and right well did they reciprocate it ten years later, when the Company alone provided one thousand pounds weight of gunpowder for Her Majesty's service. Again in 1601, during the war with Spain, the Company presented four hundred weight of gunpowder for Her Majesty's service.

It might be said that the Merchants were only contributing to the protection of their own interests, and some grounds for the assertion may be found in a minute of 1602, to the effect that a change of captains is desirable in the "shippe and pynnace" which "garde our coaste," and a messenger is sent to Mr. Jopson, the Secretary to the Admiral at Plymouth to that end, with a gift of twenty pounds, or more if necessary, for his friendship.

XXXIV.
The endless difficulties with Spain up to the time of the dispersion of the Armada would, in themselves, occupy a volume. Accounts were continually being made up between the two countries, without ever coming to a settlement. In 1572 the western Merchants were ordered to give the Queen's Commissioners, sitting in Guildhall, London, knowledge of all the injuries, personal and material, they had suffered from the King of Spain and his subjects, that restitution might be made. During the few months prior to the Spanish invasion the business was very active in this particular.

XXXV.
The Inquisition seized British sailors in Spanish ports, and endeavoured to convert them by force or by torture, the Queen vainly protesting that the deck of an English ship was English soil. Reprisals were natural enough and perhaps encouraged, and anything Spanish was considered legitimate prey. It is rather to the credit of our Merchants, that, at a time when a Spaniard was looked upon as the child of the devil, they should vote the sum of five shillings towards the burial of a poor Spaniard killed in a fray at Dartmouth.

"vijth June 1580. At this Courte it is ordered that o'
N

Appendix Threasorer this yeare shall paye unto oure Governor Mr. Phillipp Yarde xxs for somoche laid owte by him for charges to and amongst certen Spanyardes which were latelie taken by rovers out of the harbo' of Dartmouth : and their shipp and goodes taken from them, and they put a land, having nothing left."

XXXVI. Strange to say not a word is to be found in reference to the chief event of the time—the expedition of the great Armada against this country. In making up an account of the wrongs sustained at the hands of the Spaniards, there is mention of the injuries inflicted " by the Holy Howst as they term it," but this is all. We know that the Merchants of Exeter did, at that time, contribute their fair share towards the defence of the country, but there is no mention of it in the minutes of the Guild.

XXXVII. It will be remembered that early in the history of the Guild, the Adventurers opened a trade with Spain, and trafficked in raisins and wine. In 1577 overtures were made by the London Company " trading Spain and Portingall," to establish a similar Guild in Exeter. This appears to have been done, and a charter granted, the members being taken chiefly from the old Company. Probably they kept their own books and records, so we find no account of their proceedings further than that they paid fifty shillings a year for the use of the Merchants' Hall.[1]

The record is interesting in this respect, that there is no mention of such a Company in the published histories of Exeter; and it may fairly be inferred that the extensive and important trade between the west country and Spain, which exists to the present day, owes its permanence and success, if not its origin, to this Spanish Guild.

Those sympathizers with the Merchants in their supposed afflictions and oppressions, would naturally look to the customs duties as the means employed for easing them of their hard earned gains.

[1] See page 33.

CUSTOM DUTIES.

Appendix There is not in our record a single complaint or remonstrance until the year 1591, when combined action is taken on the part of the western Merchants to prosecute a suit for the "mittigating" of customs duties on woollen cloths. Mr. William Martin, the Mayor, appears to have entered upon the business at first single handed, and to have expended £305 out of his own pocket.[1] The bold attitude assumed by the Merchants probably led to a satisfactory compromise. In 1600, too, the heavy expenses of the war with Spain necessitated the imposition of a new custom

XXXVIII. to be continued for four years on the export of cloth, but again the Merchants protested against the tax in itself, and the time for which it was to be continued. The last we find of this suit is contained in a minute dated 19 February 1601.

"19 Feb. 1601. At this Courte it is agreed that Mr. Governor and Mr. Hughe Crossinge shall ride to Dorchester Assizes of purpose to conferr with Mr. Recorder of Exeter and the Officers of Weymouth concerninge a new custome of late raised uppon wollen clothes, transported for ffraunce outwarde and for all other marchaundizes homewardes. And further the whole Companie doe agree to paie two thirdes towardes their charges not onelie for a iorney by them of late made to Weymouth as also for this iorney to Weymouth and Dorchester."

There is also an imposition of 10s a tun upon Gascon wines towards the provision of Her Majesty's house (1595) which Mr. Mainwaring offers to discharge for £115 paid down, which sum

XXXIX. was readily subscribed and the duty got rid of. Customs abuses occupying a few lines, and a complaint against excessive Alnegers' fees in two short minutes, make up the sum total of

XL. the grievous exactions during a period of forty years! It is only fair, however, to read an entry which might, to prejudiced minds, throw some light on the subject, and account in some measure for the rarity of complaints.

[1] See Appendix IX.

Appendix "And where o' saide Governo' Mr. Yarde by the appointment of the Companye hath delivered unto the customer certen loves of suger to the value of iij$l$ vij$s$ xd, yt is ordered that our threasorer this yeare shall paye hym xxxij$s$ xd thereof: and the threasorer of the Spanishe Companie shall paye hym xl$s$. vij June 1580."

History tells us that Sir Walter Raleigh had certain mercantile privileges conceded to him by the Queen, *i.e.*, he was granted permission to export cloth from Exeter; he had the Vintner's licences, and certain Customs' perquisites. These concessions of themselves would cause him to be held in no great regard by the Merchants, but I think we may infer, from what little is recorded of him in our minutes, that he was anything but a favorite with them.

XLI. At the Court held 15th April 1586, a defence is instituted against Sir Walter Raleigh and his officers for the taking away of the excessive fees upon cockets and certificates. In the following month, Sir Robert Dennys, Recorder of the City, is
XLII. entreated to sit on behalf of the Company on the commission touching Sir Walter Raleigh.

Two years later, returning heart-sick and weary from an unsuccessful expedition to the west, he offered the benefit of all his discoveries in America, retaining one-fifth of the profits, to our Merchant Adventurers, and was met with this rebuff "that
XLIII. they nor anie of them woulde consent thereunto nor put their handes and seales to the said instrument for divers and sundrie speciall causes then alleged."

This is all that is recorded of the great Sir Walter, but it is significant, and indicates that there was but little sympathy for the great discoverer, and no confidence in his adventures. Not so with his half brothers—the Gilberts—as will presently be shown.

Who does not know the name of John Davis, and what schoolboy has not the name of Davis's straits geographically impressed

Appendix on his memory? This bold navigator and persevering adventurer was the first to endeavour practically to solve the theory of the North-west passage through North America to the Pacific Ocean, which has since cost so many valuable lives, and which, at this present time, occupies the attention of more than one nation.

It may not be generally known how closely John Davis[1] and his expeditions were connected with our citizens. Our minutes reveal much information on the subject, and as an introduction an extract from Hackluyt (vol. iii, p. 129) is quoted.

"The letters patents of the Queene's Majestie granted to Master Adrian Gylbert and others, for the search and discovery of the North-west Passage to China.

"Elizabeth, &c. Forasmuch as our trustie and well beloved subject Adrian Gilbert of Sandridge, in the Countie of Deuon, Gentleman, to his great costes and charges, hath greatly and earnestly trauelled and sought, and yet doth trauell and seeke, and by divers meanes indeuoureth and laboureth, that the passage unto China and the Iles of the Moluccas, by the north-westward, northeastward, or northward, unto which part or partes of the world none of our loyall subjects have hitherto had any traffique or trade, may be discovered, knowen, and frequented by the subjects of this our Realme. 6 Feb. 1583-4."

Adrian Gilbert we see lived at Sandridge, where also dwelt John Davis. These two must often have discussed, with chart and plan, the question of the north-west passage, and Gilbert seems to have not only brought his friend to his own way of thinking, but to have made him an enthusiast in the cause. The first expedition was fitted out by Mr. Secretary Walsingham and by divers worshipful Merchants, amongst whom our Exeter men found a place, as will be seen by the following minute :—

"16 Jan., 1585. At this Courte there were certaine Articles

[1] John Davis married Faith, daughter of Sir John Fulford of Fulford, Knt., by Dorothy, daughter of Lord Bourchier Earl of Bath.

Appendix. brought in by o' deputie which were deliverd hime by Mr. Carewe Rawleigh touchinge a pretended voyage to Wyngandacoia and a noate of the marchantable and other comodities there founde, which beinge published and reade, o' deputie did move the Companie to be venturers that waie. Whereunto the Companie did answere that forasmoche as they were adventurers already with Mr. Adrian Gilbte in a voiage unto China they will not adventure anie more in anie suche voiages untill they see that voiage ended or some successe thereof."[1]

In the following June, the "Barke Sunneshine of London, 50 tunnes, and the Moonshine of Dartmouth, 35 tunnes," set sail under the command of John Davis, and after various adventures, returned home on the 30th September.

The second expedition is the one most interesting to us, as we are shown the actual stake which each adventurer had in it. The entry in the Minute Book is dated 19th April, 1586, and is as follows:

"19 April, 1586. Here ffolloweth the names of those persons that did adventure there money with Mr. Adrian Gilbte and Mr. John Davies in a voiage for the discovery of China, the siveth daie of Aprill in the xxviij yeare of the rayne of o' soverayne Ladie Elizabeth:

The merchants of Exeter contributed ... £475

Owners
- Mr. John Peryam.
- „ John Applyn.
- „ Richard Dorchester.
- „ Richard Jurden.
- „ William Easton.

[1] The pretended voyage here referred to was realized in an expedition fitted out by Sir Walter Raleigh, which set forth from Plymouth shortly afterwards, and was a genuine attempt to colonize Virginia, the native name of which was Wyngandacoia. An account of the expedition and the cause of the failure of its chief object forms the subject of a Paper read by Mr. R. W. Cotton at the Meeting of the Devonshire Association at Barnstaple in 1867.

Appendix.

			£	s.
The merchants of Totnes contributed	...	...	375	0
„ „ London „	...	...	162	10
„ „ Cullompton „	...	...	25	0
„ „ Charde „	...	...	37	10
„ „ Tiverton „	...	...	25	0
Richard Duche of Hevitree „	...	...	12	10
Symon Saunders of Taunton „	...	...	12	10
John Yonge of Axminster „	...	...	25	0
Thomas Southcott of Calverley „	...	...	12	10
Christopher Broderidge of Totnes „	...	...	12	10
			£1175	0

It will be seen that our merchants not only contributed the largest share in money, but they were also the owners of the ships.

Mr. William Sanderson, the nautical instrument maker of London, a man of great importance in his day on account of his scientific knowledge, the uncle of John Davis, had an interest also in the expedition, and no doubt fitted the ships with the expensive instruments which were necessary for the voyage.

The ship "Mermayd of 120 tunnes and a pinnesse of tenne tunnes named the North Starre, together with the Sunneshine and Mooneshine" made up the little fleet which sailed from Dartmouth on the 7th May 1586. John Davis announced his return from this voyage in a letter to his uncle Sanderson, dated Exon, 14th October 1586, but the little "pinnesse" never came home.

A few words in the last minute on this subject shows that the object of our Merchants was to open a legitimate trade with China and India in the cloth, for which Devonshire was celebrated.

Appendix   A third and last expedition was fitted out and sailed in May 1587, in which, if our Exeter Merchants adventured, there is no record of the fact: that it was proposed to and considered by them appears from the following minutes :—

"16th Dec. 1587. Also at the same Courte there was reade a coppie of certaine articles under divers of the Companies handes concerninge a newe adventure with Mr. Adrian Gilberte and Mr. John Davyes to China and Cathay, whereuppon Mr. Governo' did move the whole Companie what they intended to do therein, and praied there resolute answere, who agreed that Mr. Nicholas Martyn, Mr. Nicholas Spicer, Mr. Sampforde, Mr. Hackwell and Mr. Jasper Horssey, shall consider of all the accomptes of the voiage heretofore made by the said Adrian Gilbte and John Davies, and shall also set downe what they think fit to be answered to the said articles with as much speade as conveyniently they maie, which said articles and lres were by Mr. Governo' delivered to Mr. Sampforde in open Courte."

"15 Feb. 1588. It is ordered by the companie then presente, that Mr. Nicholas Spicer, John Hackwill, Richard Dorchester, and Jasper Horssey should deale with Mr. William Martyn for the examination of the accomptes of the last voiage in the Marmaide to China, and that the same be brought in orderly made at the next courte; and also to enquire of a ballet of cloth reported to be missinge, that restitucion maie be made unto every adventurer accordinge to the p'porcon of the same."

The traces of Davis are still to be found in the map of North America by the local names which he gave to the various places he discovered. On sighting first the land, he named the bay which he entered after his friend, Gilbert Sound; we find, also, Exeter Sound, Totnes Roads, Mount Raleigh, and other familiar titles. A few years later, John Davis found the right course to India and China, and introduced the trade from this county which exists to the present time.

Appendix. There is another name, a household word with Devonians, concerning which we have some little information. Scant though it be, every scrap relating to Sir Humphrey Gilbert is of interest and ought to be preserved.

"4th Jan. 1583. At this Courte ther is a lre reade from the right wor' Sr Fraunces Walsingham, Knight, chief Secretary to her Matie, dated the viijth daye of December 1582, directed to the Maior of Exeter, touching the voyage pretended to the westren parte of America by Sr Humfrye Gilbert, Knight, and others.

"Also ther is an other lre reade from the right wor' Sir George Peckham, Knight, dated the xiiijth December 1582, directed also to the saide Maio' of Exeter, touching the saide matter.

"And this Courte being especiallie called to understande what money everie one of this Companye will disburse and adventure in and aboute the settinge forth of certen shippinge to the saide parties of America; and the Governo' moving the Companye thereunto and declared the greate benefite and commoditie thereof ensuying: The whole generallitie doo lyke well of the saide voyage and wysh good successe therunto, and woulde be glade to adventure and set forth shipping thether: But considering the tyme of the yeare to be ffarr spente for preparation of shippinge and provision for suche a voyage, they mynde to respecte thereupon this yeare; and the next yeare as they shall see success therein, they will be glade to adventure thether and doo anything for the furtherance thereof."

"Memorandu: that the xith daye of January 1583, one Olyver Manwayringe, servant to the right wo' Sr George Peckham, Knight, being authorized for that purpose, came in and declared the pretence and order of a voyage pretended to the westren parte of America, and the greate benefite and commoditie that may ensue thereof, as well to the whole realme as to the Adventurers that waye: And shewed forth certen lres

Appendix: patente for the assurance of the benefitte of the said Adventurers, and a booke touching the description and order of the saide pretended voyage : Whereuppon the 'Governor moved the Companye to set forth certen shipping, and to be Adventurers that waye : But forasmoche as ther is two lres directed to the Maio' of Exon : one from the right wo' Sr Fraunces Walsingham, Knight, chief Secretary to her Matie, and thother from the saide Sr George Peckham touching the saide matter, the Governo' Consulls, and Companye thought it good that the Maio' and Aldermen his bretheren should conferr as well for the answering of their saide wo' lres, as also to take order for shipping and adventuring in the saide voyage."

" 30 Jany, 1583. This courte being especiallie called to understande what everie one of this companye would adventure to the foresaide parties of America : and the Governo' moving them thereunto (Olyver Manwayring being present) the parties whose names are hereunder writen dyd agree and promise to adventure everie of them to the setting forth of a shipp that waye as hereafter followeth, viz.,

Mr. Nicholas Martyn	... ...	xii$l$ xs
Mr. Thomas Martyn	. . ...	xii$l$ xs
Mr. George Smyth	... ...	xii$l$ xs
Mr. Thomas Spicer	... ...	xii$l$ xs
John Hoyle ...	... ...	xii$l$ xs
Richard Jordeyne	... ...	xii$l$ xs
Myles Lambert	... ...	xii$l$ xs"

These records reveal to us information of a melancholy interest ; they show the confidence our merchants had in the great Sir Humfrye Gilbert ; they contain a warning which he would have done well to have heeded, and though rightly mistrusting the prudence of the adventure, they would not withhold assistance. History tells us what important results arose from this expedition, and history tells us the pathetic story of the disasters

Appendix which overtook it; how in the little craft, 'The Squirrel,' of only ten tons, the great general resolved to make his way home; how his officers did all in their power to persuade him to enter the larger vessel, the 'Golden Hind,' and his reply "that he would never desert the bark nor the crew with whom he had encountered so many dangers;" and how on the ninth of September in the evening, in the midst of a great tempest, Sir Humphrey was seen sitting in the stern of his ship with his book, and was often heard by the crew of the 'Hind' to say with a loud voice, " Courage, my lads! we are as near heaven at sea as by land." How about midnight the little ship went down and was no more seen ; and so perished as noble, gallant, and beloved a gentleman as any who lived in those times, prolific in great characters.

There are two letters read to the court from Sir Francis Drake—it is a pity they are not copied *verbatim*—touching the Quixotic expedition to take Portugal from the Spaniards, and set the exiled king on the throne. The minutes of October 1588, and February 1589 merely record the reading of the letters, and the absence of any comment upon them is significant of what our merchants thought of the adventure.

" 30 Oct. 1588. At this Courte ther was reade a lre dyrected from Sr Fraunces Drake, knyght, to the gentilmen Merchauntes and inhabitauntes of this cittie to adventure with hime and one Sr John Norris in a voiage supportinge some speciall service for her Matie for the defence of o' religion, Quene and countrye, dated the 17th October, 1588; together with the order and manner of a warrant for suche as will adventure howe they shalbe assured of suche monyes as they shall adventure, dated the 18th of October 1588."

" 31st Feb. 1589. At this Courte ther was one other lre directed from S' Ffraunces Drake, Knight, to the Maior and Aldermen of the Cittie of Exon, touchinge an adventure with

Appendix. hime and others in a voiage for her Maties service, dated the — of January 1588 (*o.s.*) 1589."

In these days of unrestricted intercourse with other nations we can scarcely realize a state of affairs, which would render it almost impossible to obtain corn, wherewith to make bread, at any price. That this was the case may be learned from contemporary documents. In Philip Wyott's diary, before alluded to, we find that in 1586 Justices sat and gave direction that no corn should go abroad but be kept for the maintenance of the poor in every parish, and that persons should be appointed " to view barnes and mows and to take a note what store of corn there was, and what people were in such houses as had corne to spare, and allowing evy pson a peck a weke to certify the overplus to the said Justices." Wheat at this time was eight shillings, rye six shillings, and barley five shillings and eight pence a bushel.

From a minute in March 1586, it appears that the Company had sent for a cargo of corn from some foreign port for the relief of the city; but a month later, so great had the scarcity become, it was necessary to see to themselves as well as the poor, and they resolved that every subscriber of one pound should have a bushel of wheat and a bushel of rye towards the redemption of his contribution.

XLIV. Another decade brought with it a recurrence of famine. In 1596, still indebted to Philip Wyott's diary for the information, we find that "all this May hath not been a dry day or night." Again in June and in August there is the chronicle of "continual rains," and later on, "not a dry day in November." It says something for the foresight of our Merchants that, in August of this year, considering that "corne was like to growe dearer rather than better cheape by meanes of the ffowle weather," they should seek to import from foreign countries the precious grain which their own land would, to all appearances, fail to yield them.

Nos. 19 and 20, North Street.

THE FAMINE.   89

Appendix. The mode of administering relief to the citizens and the poor was ingenious, and is worthy of note. Rye at that time was selling, as a favor, at nine shillings the bushel. The cargo was purchased at the rate of four shillings and sixpence a bushel. One third of the amount disbursed by a Member of the Company was delivered to him in kind, for his own use or to make what he could of it, the remaining two-thirds in value was sold to poor householders and the poor at the cost price.

XLV. In the early spring of the following year, the prospects became worse, continued rains prevented both the sowing and the gathering of the wheat. So soon as February 1597, energetic action was taken by the Company to prevent a great calamity. The noble sum of £550 was, without hesitation, subscribed in order to provide the city with the first necessary of life; and the advantage of thus taking early steps to insure a supply of corn is evidenced in the fact that they were enabled to sell it at 5s 8d. a bushel, when the market price was more than double.

That the Company were regarded, not merely as a trading body, but as representatives of the social life of the city, is shown by the circumstance that three widows subscribed handsomely towards this fund.

XLVI. There are other instances of the charitable disposition of the Company which may fitly be introduced here. The petition of Philipp Cane is a well written and manly appeal for help under adverse circumstances, and the response indicates that the case was deserving of consideration.

In our local history there is an account given of the "Black Assize" which was held in the spring of 1586. It was so called from the fearful mortality which followed the trial of certain prisoners who brought the gaol fever into Court, and of those who were present, ten magistrates, eleven jurymen, and a great number of constables and others fell victims to this terribly contagious disease. The fever was generated by certain prisoners

Appendix who were taken from a Portuguese ship, homeward bound from Newfoundland with fish, by Barnard Drake, Esquire, and who were maintained in a most miserable condition in the gaol. This gentleman is described in the historical record of his death as Sir Barnard Drake, Knt., and as he was a magistrate present at the trial, and one of the first to succumb to the fever, it almost appears like a retribution, which would have been intensified if he obtained his knighthood, as is not improbable, for this very exploit.[1]

XLVII. The attention of the Company was directed to the case of these unfortunate prisoners some time previously, and their necessities relieved.

XLVIII. In the year 1593 the front of the Guildhall was rebuilt, and behind the portico—on the site occupied by the present police offices—an open room or corridor was constructed. Towards the expense of this work our Company contributed forty pounds for "paving, seelinge, stoves and winscott."

This corridor, we learn from a side note, was used as a "walke;" and we can imagine the stately old Merchants in starched ruff, doublet and hose, refreshing themselves at the close of day with promenade and social gossip; whilst the strains of music proceeding from the cool and airy situation of the "leddes of the Guildhalde" would show that they were not indifferent to the softer arts.

"13 Dec. 1593. At this Courte Mr. Governo' did move the whole Companie concerninge a yearly fee to be geven frome hensforthe to the waites of this Cittie, whereunto the whole Companie agreed. And thereuppon Mr. Governo' did put it to triall of handes whether they shoulde have yearly a xxvj*s* viiij*d* or a xl*s*, whereuppon the whole Companie agreed, that they

---

[1] Sir Bernard Drake was knighted by Queen Elizabeth at Greenwich in 1585. He died April 10th 1586, and was buried in the parish Church of Musbury, Devon.

shoulde have yearly ffortie shillings at the pleasure of this Companie, the firste payment to begynne at the ffeaste of the Birthe of o' Lorde God next ensewinge, and to be paied yearly by the Treasorer of this Companie for the tyme beinge. And in consideracon thereof the said waites do promis to plaie evrye sundaie and holy daie betwene the ffeaste of Saincte Michaell tharchangell and the ffeaste of thannunciacon of o' Ladie beinge in the wynter one quarter of an hower before supper tyme uppon the leddes of the Guilhalde, and betwene the said ffeaste of thannunciacon and the ffeaste of St. Michaell beinge in the somer tyme halfe of an hower."

"6 Sept. 1597. At this Courte it is agreed that from hensfourthe there shalbe paid yearlie by our Tresorer to Medlandes boy beinge one of the waits, tenne shillinges to thende that he and the reste shall amend there musicke and continewe the time in playenge uppon the leddes of the Guilhald as in a former Act is mencioned."

XLIX. So early as the year 1580, the attention of the Company was directed to the desirability of appointing a public preacher and religious instructor, and they were invited to support the Mayor by contributing something towards a stipend for a functionary to be instituted for those purposes, but nothing seems to have been done on that occasion. In 1599, the subject was again brought up by the Governor of the Company, and a motion was carried

L. that ten pounds a year should be paid as a contribution for and "towardes the restablishinge of the Catachisme and procuringe of a learned preacher within this Citie the better to instruct the people in the knowledge of God." Some disagreement as to the mode of raising the money delayed the appointment for more

LI. than twelve months, when the Corporation and the Company agreed to the appointment of the Rev. Edmond Snape, D.D., to the office, at a salary of £50 a year.

Among the municipal records is the following document:—

Appendix. "21 August 1600. The Chamber to Edmond Snape counterpart of appointment as a preacher in Exeter, to preach twice a week, viz., on the Sabbath day at 6 a.m., and in the afternoon, with a salary of £50."

"Signed Edmond Snape."

Seal : a death's head, hour glass and book, with initials E.S.

In Fuller's "Worthies" on the subject 'Cotton,' temp. 1599, the following curious note occurs :—

"Mr. Snape a second Cartwright (not for abilities but activity) came out of Jersey, and plentifully sowed the seeds of Non-conformity in his Diocesse, which the vigilancy of this stout and prudent Prelate plucked up by the roots, before they could come to perfection."

Can it be possible that the public preacher and this Nonconformist were one and the same person?

The remaining few extracts are arranged in chronological order. The resolution respecting the apprentice, Richard Newman, is illustrative of the interest taken by the Guild in those who would, in good time, become members, and whose education consequently was a matter of some importance.

LII.

The order that dilatory arbitrators should be fined, arose out of a reluctance on the part of certain gentlemen to decide in a case where John Davy (who was a man of no small consequence) had been presented for calling John Twose "drunken beast, which are onseemlie wordes." The gentle pressure of a fine probably had the effect of compelling the appointed to carry out a disagreeable duty. The next extract is a proclamation against the wearing of sumptuous apparel, aimed not so much at the extravagance and immoral tendency of the practice, as against purchasing the fine goods of the hateful foreigner, to the neglect of our own more homely, if more useful fabrics.

LIII.

LIV.

".Merchauntes who do dwell in villages or uplandish townes" would have this advantage over their brethren in cities, in that

THE BROAD GATE (INTERIOR).

MISCELLANEOUS.

Appendix LV. they could do pretty much as they liked, without fear of the intervention of the Guild, in those days of restricted intercourse. Hence the desire to prevent young adventurers from starting in life, on their own account, free from the wholesome restrictions which they would be subject to under the eye of the Guild.

LVI. An attempt to infringe upon the liberties of the Company by some Merchants of Taunton appears to have resulted in failure, and entailed a liability, in respect of the expenses consequent upon resenting the offence.

LVII. Probably one of the first exercising the calling of a broker was appointed by the Company in 1593, but it could not have been a very profitable office, as his commission was but two pence in the pound, and that he was to divide, if another broker came upon the scene on the opposite side.

LVIII. During the same year one Robert Petter, feltmaker, was discovered to be doing a little contraband business in "Whitware" from Pampoole, having contrived to bring home five or six yards in the "Pleasure" of Topsham. The next year getting bold by success, he brought home fourteen yards and a half in the "Mary of Jarsey." This was too much for the feelings of the Guild, so he was speedily called to account, and suffered for his offences.

LIX. A case of shuffling, as to the ownership of certain goods upon which a distress appears to have been levied, was thoroughly sifted in the matter of William Tucker, who occasioned some trouble and expense, but ultimately got the worst of it.

LX. The refusal of Thomas Chaffe to submit to the formalities usual in the admission to the Guild, for conscience sake, is curious, but the excuse alleged is so "ffryvolous" that there was probably some other motive lurking beneath, which might have been suspected by the Court, and acted upon accordingly.

The disturbed state of the Channel during the continuous struggles for supremacy, between English, French, Dutch, and

P

Appendix LXI.

Spanish, at the close of the century, is shown in the minutes relating to the Dunkirks. From the port of Dunkirk a band of free rovers hailed, who, taking advantage of the troublous times, infested the coasts, and under cover of letters of mark (not infrequently forged) committed sad depredations upon peaceful merchantmen.

LXII.

In 1602, when the siege of Ostend fully occupied the attention of the Spaniards, whose ships would be constantly passing up and down channel, there is some complaint of negligence on the part of the guardships. Probably the Captains were more intent on the larger prey offered in the Spanish vessels, and allowed the little rovers opportunities which they would not be slow to seize. After fitting out the "Katherine" on their own account with gunpowder and "furniture," the Merchants sent a deputation to the Secretary to the Admiralty at Plymouth, with authority to secure his good will and "frendshippe" by an expenditure of twenty pounds, or more if necessary, the object being to get more competent captains to command the warships. Two names are suggested for appointment, the Mayor of Plymouth and the famous Captain Sonds.

LXIII.

Towards the latter part of the century there was a great accession of members, as many as ten being admitted at one Court; the advantages derivable from the connexion during this prosperous period, no doubt inducing many to abandon their own professions and join the more lucrative one of "Merchaundize." The regulations for admission in all cases were stringently enforced, both with those who claimed entrance by right, and those who like Mr. Newcombe found difficulties and a heavy fee in the way. It was a good stroke of policy on his part to obtain a letter of recommendation from Mr. Canon Leach, who (as he doubtless knew) was a favorite with the Merchants. Mr. Roberts tells us that "about 1610 the Chamber of Exeter used to vote sugar-loaves to Mr. Canon Bodley and Mr. Canon Leach, in

Appendix token of their approbation of their pains taken in the morning lecture at St. Peter's."

These notes will be appropriately brought to a conclusion with the Treasurer's balance-sheet. It is dated early in the history of the Guild, and singularly enough is the only one to be met with throughout the minutes. The cash accounts, however, of so important a corporation, as it grew in strength, would be kept in a separate book.

"The accopte of William Waye, Threasurer for the laste yeare, made before Nicholas Martyn, Harry Ellacote and John Ffelde, the xiijth daye of this present August 1566.

"The saide William Waye hath receved in money for his yeare as appereth in viij Courtes before the some of x*l* viij*s* i*d*

"Whereof he hath layed oute and payed as foloweth :—

"Ffyrst to John Ffelde for this yeares wages and for three quarters behind the last yeare	xxiij*s*	iiij*d*
Item payed to John Tooker ...	xlij*s*	
Item for a newe keye for the box ...		iiij*d*
Item payed for ij peces of gree fryse conteyning lxxij yardes	iii*l* xvj*s*	
Item paied also for a yarde of fryse ...		xxj*d*
Item payed for viij yardes of white cotten at ix*d* the yarde	vj*s*	
Item to Ralfe Sadyforth for the making of xij gonnes	ix*s*	
Item payed to x watchmen on Mydsomer nyght with drycnke	iij*s* viij*d*	
Item paied to John ffelde for wrytinge this booke	xx*s*	

Sum. ix*l* ij*s* j*d*

"Soo remayneth due to the Howse xxvj*s*, which xxvj*s* was delivered to Nicholas Martyn at the levelinge of this accompte."

p²

ADDENDUM.

The Mr. Doctor Tremayne referred to at page 60 was a D.D., Canon Residentiary, and Treasurer of the Cathedral. He was an excellent preacher, and died in 1584. His elder brother Edward, one of the Clerks of the Council, had an honorary salary settled on him by the City of Exon, for the good offices which they had received and expected.—*Moore's History of Devonshire.*

Protest against Excessive Duties.

"11 Feb. 1602. Also at this Courte Mr. Governo' did move the whole Companie whether they woulde yeilde to paie the rate demaunded by Andrewe Cholwill, gent., deputie unto Mr. Symon Harvey, upon spices, sugars, &c., the particulers beinge sett downe as ffolloweth, viz., uppon

Pepper, mace, cloves, Nutmeggs, synymonn } the hundred weight		ijs
Sugar the hundred		xijd
Prunes the puncheon		iiijd
Reasons the pece		ijd
Reasons of the the hundred		vjd
ffiges the barrell or tapett		ijd
Currantes the tonne		ijs
Dates the hundred		xijd
Almondes the hundred		xijd
Annys Seade the hundred		xijd
Lecoras the hundred		xijd
Rise the hundred		vjd
Sope the hundred		vjd
Oyle the tonne		vjs viijd
Olives the tonne		iijs
honye the tonne		iijs
Sugar the chest		xijd
Sugar in loves the chest		ijd
Sugar in loves refined that use to come in ffates the hundred		xijd
Molasses the tonne		ijs

"Whereuppon the whole Companie doe agree that frome hensfforth the said rate shall not be paid by anie of this Companie to the said Symon Harvey or anie of his deputie or deputies, and that Mr. John Ellacott Governo', Mr. Willm. Martyn, Mr. John Howell, Mr. Dorchester, Mr. Willm. Spicer, Mr. John Prouse, Mr. Willm. Martyn, Councellor, Mr. Hugh Crossinge, John Sandey, Robert Parr, and Henry Sweete, or sixe of them, shall betwene this and the next Courte drawe and penne an acte concerninge the foresaid premisses, and certifie the same at the next Courte followinge."

APPENDIX.

I.

The Oration or Declaration which I, John Vowell al's Hoker, made by the appoyntment of Mr. Robert Mydwynter Maior unto the Comons of the Citie of Exon at the Guildhall the xxvth of Januarie 1559.

"My Masters, the cause why yo are called hether at these presents is to notifie unto yo the tenner of certeyne lres and a decree which the Queenes Maties most honorable Council hath sent unto o Masters Mr. Maior and his brethren, as touching an order by their honors taken for thapeasinge of the late controversie among us: most hartely pyenge us all quietly and paciently to geve care thereunto: The effecte of them consysteth in too poyntes—thone concerninge obedience and thother touching concorde and unitye, which too are of suche force and effycacie, that therby all comonwelthes and all estates are preserved and kept, and without them all are turned to utter ruyn and desolacion, whereof to declare pticularly it may apeer by many and sundrie examples how that thobedience of the people hath not onelie bene moste acceptable before God, but hath also bene the most assured staye and preservacion of them in all ages and tymes. Whereas controverslye disobedience moste displeaseth God and procureth his heavie hande againe us: yea and so haynest and displeasinge is the same in his sight that even from the fyrst begyning he opened it when he showed his hevie displeasure in revenging thereof. Ffor when Adam was fyrst made and created and apoynted the Lorde and Governo' of all the workes of God, which were all made to serve his use, God wylled him that in no wyse he sholde touche or eate of the aple of the tree of lyffe and dethe which then dyd growe in the middle of the garden of Paradise: but Adam forgeting his deutye wolde needs taste and eate therof: the smarte whereof he forthwh felte and not he alone but all his posteritie all beinge exiled out of that garden: and man wolde thinke it but a smale mater to taste or eate of an aple speciallie the same beinge made for manne and whereof was such abundance and plentie as a mannes seeing the lacke of one coulde not be so greate a mater: Yet God who requireth not so moche of us obedience as doth abhorr disobedience doth not onely exile Adam and Eva his wyffe but all his posteritie out from the garden of innocencie wh wee all do yet at these presente feele—lykewyse the children of Israell when they forgetinge there obedience dyd murmur agayn Moyses and Aaron because they had not fleshe to eate in the wilderness as they were wonte to have in Egipt allthough God gave them there own desyres and rayned downe from heaven bothe quayles and manna, yet let he not unrevenged ne yet unplayned there former disobedience but even whyles the meate was yet in there mouthes his countenance was moved agayn them and slew them wh an exceding great plague. Also Corathe Dathan and Abyron were miche offended wh Moyses and Aaron and repyned against them, but what folowed even they when they thought to offer incense to God he nothing accepting the same the earthe opened and swalowed up bothe theyme there houses and all the people that were with them: yea and as the historie saiethe they all went downe alyve in to hell.

Absolon also Kinge Davids sone who was right deere unto his father and who coulde wante nothinge yeat wheyn he gave to mislyke the Government of his and wolde needes be Kinge him selfe and rule after his owne mynde it do so move and displease God that he rooted him out from of the face of the earthe, for Absolon riding upon his horse under an oke was hanged by the heare of his hedde and there dyd so hange untill one Joab came and slew him. Many other examples there be both in the sacred as also in the prophane histories, as especiallie in the chronicles of this realme, wch may well shew unto us the frute of contempte and disobedience of the higher powers, whereof some have been seene even by many now yet alive and here present beinge the same done as well in the tymes of Kinge Henry the vijth, Henry the viijth, Edward the vjth, as also in the tyme of Queene Marie. Ffor when certeyn men, mislyking the Government of Kinge Henry the vijth dyd cluster themselves together, and under the guydinge of one called the blackesmithe, came from the mounte to this Citie and from thence to London, and then to Blackhethe felde redy wh force to prevayle wh the Kinge: What followed bysydes the shedinge of bloodd? The plague was upon them and there posteritie.

Lykewise when in the tyme of King Henry the viijth certeyn of the northe countrie myslyked the affayres and doinges of the Kynge and dyd congregate themselves to repyne his attemptes, even, as it was thought, of a verie zeale and love to God, yet it is well known what a plague and what an evell successe folowed the same.

In the tyme of Kinge Edward the vjth the vulgare people and comones of these west countries having, as they saide, a zeale in goode cause, could not abyde the reformacon of the prince in causes of religion: Wherefor they clustered themselves together, chose to themselves certeyn captaynes and lay here about this Citie as yo know a long tyme. But alas in thende thereof how was there bloode spylt, there goodes wasted, and both they and there posteritie brought to utter reproche, confusion and shame. And fynallye, now of late in the tyme of Queene Marye it is not unknown how Sr Thomas Wyat, even of a verie zeale to defend the nacion and to preserve it the libertie thereof from the overuning of the strange nacions, dyd aryse in defense thereof: but alas yo know what an evell successe God gave thereunto, and how the plague lighted upon him to the confusion of him selfe and reproche of his prosteritie. Ffor assuredlie such is the displeasure of God agayn suche as shall repyne the prime magistrate and higher powers, that be the cause never so good in our sighte, yet before God it is so displeasant that he will not leave it unpunished: the cause he taketh to be his owne, and therefore upon him selfe taketh he the revenge thereof: the state of higher powers is as deere unto him as the aple of his eye which nowise will he to be touched.

Wherefore let us all well remember, as well for the dewtie we owe unto God, the obedience unto the prince and love to this our Comon welthe and Citie that wh all humbleness and obedience wee do quietlie submitt our selfs to the Government of the higher powers and magistrates.

Q

And as I have thus spoken of obedience, so thinke ye the same of concord, love and unitie; for without it be the blessinge of God otherwise never so great and manyfolde unto us yet shall not the same availe us but rather rebownde to o' confusion, for suche is the nature of love and concorde that by it smale and weake thinges become to be greate, mightie and stronge, and of the contrarie by discorde and division most puissant and strong matters have become feble and weke and of no force nor effecte.

Ffor wheresoever love, concorde and unitie are not there is all disorder and confusion. Esop therefore hathe a fable that one a tyme there was a contention between the bodie and the membres of the same,—the membres forgeating in what a unitie they were knitt unto the bodie beganc to murmure and grudge, the hande refusing to do his function, the foote being werie to do his vocation : and finally everie membre forgeting in what an unitie he was compacte and ioyned in the bodie, swerved from doinge his dewtie and part. Thus the bodie beinge divided everie one membre having smale regarde of thother were at length brought to suche a feeble and extreme state that they awayted for nothinge but even the utter decaye and confusion of them selves wh indeed folowed, even so shall it be by us : for when everie singuler membre envieng the state of the bodie will of any singuler fantasie swerve from that unitie we are all conjoined in lett him awayte most assuredlie for destruction. Ffor as he beinge knytt and joyned to the bodye shall seele his owne preservacion and contynuance so beinge severed shall as a member without sustenance be brought to confusion and decaye.

Ffor concord and unitie preserveth and kepeth whereas discord and division destroicthe and subvertethe. Wherefore one Scyturus a Scythian borne beinge one stryken in yeres and having xxx sones alyve to pswade them to a concorde love and unitie amonge them selfes used this familier example : he caused a lytle before his dethe a fagott to be made of so many styckes as he had children and the same being sett before him he called all his sones before him and commanded theldest to take the fagott and to break it, wh when he coulde not do, then he willed the seconde to do it and then the iij and so finallie averic one one after another : and when none of them coulde breake the fagott he willed the eldest sone to take out a stycke and breake it wch when he had done he willed the seconde to do so and so from one to another the lyke he commanded. Wch when everie one of them had done and broken hys stycke then thus he saide unto them: even thus shall it be wh yo' for as long as ye shall contynew together within the compasse and bonde of love and unitie ye shall be strong and invincible: but if any one of yo' fleete and swerve from a nother and be ones out of the fagott and be at variance discorde and contention then shall yo' be weake feble and easie to be broken and overthrowen which his sayeinge is not so wise as most trew: for it is a rule among the philosophers "omnis virtus unita magis in se valet quam dispersa." Everie thinge wch hathe any vertewe is of muche more force and effecte when it is ioyned together in one, than when it is dispersed and devyded: wch to be most trew hathe apered by many examples in the comon welthe of this o' Citie: who when we have ioyned together in one hert, one mynde and one bodye have ben of suche force as agayne whom our adversaries and enemies have but smallie prevayled ffor in the xlvjth yere after the incarnacion of Christ wch were about xxiiij yeres before the destruction of Jerusalem Claudius the empero' sent Vespasian then Duke of his armye in to this realme and here beinge with a mightie hoast beseged this Citie whose puyssance and might thoughe coulde not be withstanded by so smale a company as in respecte of his were within the Citie yet dyd the inhabitants so ioyne themselves together in one herte and one mynde with such a fyrme concorde and unitie that thempero' being not hable to prevayle was enforced to rayse his sege yea and as some saye fayne to take the seas for his succo'.

Lykewyse in the tyme of King Edwarde the iiijth thoughe it be storie to all men not knowen yet treu it is that sundry of the nobilitie of this realme taking parte wh King Edwarde lay and harbored within this Citie: others of the nobilitie then bearing and taking parte wh Kinge Henry the vjth nothing pleased therewith assembled themselfes together and with an army beseged this Citie: at wh tyme the Citizens were in greate perplexities the nobilitie who were within requiring to have the keyes of the Citie in their custodie and to have the government of the Citie, and the nobylitie lykewise wch were without by force seekinge to prevaile, but in this extremitie the Citizens ioined them selfes so fyrmly in unitie and concorde together that as they gave no place nether graunted to other pt. so dyd they preserve the Citie from daunger and invasion. And finally last of all wee wch are here now present do well know in what a miserable state this Citie and we o' selfes were in at the last comocion beinge one everie syde environed with our enemies: and yet being fyrmely ioyned together in unitie and concorde dyd prevaile agayne them, ffor certeinglie such is the force and nature of love and unitie as whereby all things are preserved and contynewed even as by division contencion and discorde cometh utter confusion and desolacion. There hath of late benne a controversie and variaunce amonge us wch hath bredd miche unquietness: the same hath bene opened and referred to the honorable o' good Lordes of the Queene's Maties Councell: who tendering the state of us and of o' comon welthe have wh no smale paynes travelled to reduce the same to a quiett and finall determinacion, and lykewise they have of ther honores sent the same to o' master the maior and his brethren here present wh there lres, requiring us all wh quietness to obey and observe the same. They shalbe thearfore openlie playnelie and distynctlie redde unto yo' praienge yo' to geve attente care thereunto and to beare it well awaie.

And then I toke the lres and fyrst I dyd reede them playnlie and distynctlie, that done I dyd reede everie sentence by sentence repeting everie one once or twice: that done I tooke thorder and when I had redden it once over I saide this—

My masters ye knowe the controversie amonge us was cheeflye for ij causes thone touching buyinge and sellinge of marchandyse by retayle, and thother for adventuring beyonde the seas. For the fyrst the wisedome of the honorable Councell wayeinge and consyderinge o' estate, have not thought good the lybertie of buyeinge and sellinge by retayle sholde be restrayned from any maner of citezen or inhabitant within this citie of what condicion or degree he be of: but to have his free lybertie and choyse to use the same at his owne will and pleasure without lett or deneall: And for the seconde arle marke there honorable wisedomes who lyke fathers of this oure comon welthe have a speciall regarde unto us—ffor forasmiche to be an adventurer is not onlie to be subjecte to the perilles of the seas, but do the also require a more exacte knowledge in it selfe then other trades dothe without whch the trade is lyke to be more daungerose then profytable, therefore there honores thinkinge not good that everie unskillfull pson sholde attempte this trade wch is more lyke to turne to his decaye then comoditie will not that any sholde attempte the trade of suche adventuringe oneles he were first skillfull therein for if any one having not skill sholde by adventuringe receve the loss the same shall not onelie be the decay of him, his wyffe his familie and his freendes but a losse to the comon welthe, he being not able to be so frutfull a member therein as he before was. There wisedomes therefore having so fatherlye a care of us wolde not wee sholde attempte the thinge wch might turne us to decaye or ruyn. And yet notwithstanding there honores exclude not everie pson from adventuring but onelie suche as are unfytt or unapte but if any wilbe an adventurer lett him sewe to be of this companye who if he be discerned and judged to be fytt for the same he shall not onelie be admitted thereunto but shall also be receved into the same Companie gratis freelie without any chardge or coste at all. And because a reasonable meane sholde be hadd in chosing and electinge of suche as be fytt, this order is taken that the Maior the Aldermen and Comon Councell of this Citie ioyning to them ten of the hedd and cheffe comoners who knowe the state of everie inhabytant within this Citie shall examyn and judge whether evereops on so seweng to be a Marchant Adventurer be fytt and meete for the same or not according to which order the saide tenne comoners be elected and chosen whose names be these (which I then rehersed and said thus): This is the order and therefore I py ye to marcke it well, I will reede it agayne once more unto yo' (and then I dyd so and thus I sayd) fforasmuch as the Queene's Maties most honorable Councell hath wh greate paynes and travelle sett and made this order it is not onelie o' bownden dewtie to receve and accepte it but also with all humbleness of hert in quiet concorde and unitie we oughte to obey the same conforming o' selves in all quiet order to th' accomplisshing thereof. And our Master the Maior and all his brethren do here before yo' all not onelie for there partes promise to obey the same but also do desyre yo' to do the lyke : And that all matters of displeasure variaunce and contencion sett apart now freendly to agree all together in all love concorde and unite wh for there partes do both crave and desire of yo' offering to ioyne wh yo' wh all love and unitie. And according to thorder taken as requisitt it is they offer here that no inhabitante at all within this Citie shalbe interrupted from retaylinge of any kinde of wares and mchaundize, nether yet will refuse any man to be of the Societie of the M'chauntes but being ones iudged meete shalbe receved wh hert and mynde gratis freelie wthout any cost or charge at all : but yet understande yo' too thinges as and shalbe required of everie one admitted in to this companye wthout wh he cannot be receved : that is to saie obedience to the Masters and Governors of this Company, and love and unitie one wth another for without these too he cannot be receved : Wherefore Masters as I do nothing doubte so do I trust yo' will conforme yorselves quietlie to this order : wh I do require of yo' both for the dewtie yo' owe unto God the obedience to the higher powers and regarde of this our comon welthe : I mistrust not but that yo' will conforme yorselves wh all quietness and obedyence to observe the same : ffor God commaundeth it, the prynce and higher powers require it and the state of o' comon welthe loketh for it (wh ar and sholde be sufficient arguments for everie man to quiet and content himselfe) yea and if there were ells nothing to move us unto it yet o' verie Citie and situacion of the same might sufficiently teache us what to do : ffor as ye know it is placed and situated upon an hill beinge above the whoale countrie adioyning : wh teachethe o' conversacion o' love our concorde and unitie amonge o' selves sholde be suche as that it sholde be a spectacle to the whole countrie adioyning to beholde : it is walled roundeabout wh lyme and stone, even sholde we fast ioyned one to another wh the hoate lyme of love and unitie and wh the sande of obedience wh shall better defend us then any wall of stone be it never so stronge. And therefore as it now cometh to my remembraunce when certyn ambassadores were sent from Athenes to Lacedemonia they vewinge the Citie asked where the walles were of the Citie : wherewh certyn of the citezens stepping forthe and ioyning themselves together awnsered we ar the walls of Sparta, meaning that they so agreed together in obeyinge the higher powers and suche love and unitie one wh another that no enemy was able to prevayle agayne them and that no walle could be stronger then were they beinge thus ioyned in love quietnes and obedience. The sone assone as he ariseth casteth his heate and beames of light upon us, even so sholde we evry the morninge spredd the heate and beames of unfayned love and unitie upon all o' neighbores : lykwise one showre of rayne wassheth awaye the fylthe of all o' streetes even so sholde the dewe and love of unitie washe awaye from us all contemptes all hatredes and all displeasures that nothinge be so plentyfullie remayninge amonge us as love peace and unitie. Whereby be we assured we shall most sacfflie kepe and defende this our comon welthe and best pvide for our selfes and our posteritie. And therefore yet once more I do most hartelie pray yea and require yo' all in the name of God in the name of the Prince and higher powers and in the name of the comon welth the pservacion whereof we all must tender that everie one of us do quietly conforme and aplie our-selves to thobeying and keping of thorder now taken : And if it be so that any psons not contented to do his dewtie shall travell by any maner of waies to pswade yo' to the contrarie or whisper in corners any vayne thinge wheh might withdrawe yo' from this trew unitie love and obedience beleve him not nether yet geve eare unto him : For he is therein a most unprofytable member in the comon wethe : but rather if yo' will do well dis-close and reveale him to the magistrat that according to his desertes he may receve a condigne punishment. And let us all as our deuties are castawaye from us all discorde division and discension, and lett us as brothers agree all together in love con-corde and unitie. And as God shalbe so prayed the prince reioysed and o' Citie preserved so doubte I not but the pros-peritie thereof shalbe bothe upon this Citie and upon us and o' posteritie whch the Lorde graunte unto us all.

II.

"XV May 1562. Whereas John Pyll an inhabitant of this Citie hath traffiqued oute of this realme into the domynions of Ffraunce as also hath traffiqued from the parties of ffraunce into the Citie being not free of this Companye : And therfore ther is now stayed a fardell of dowlas to answere such fyne as shalbe assessed upon hym which remayneth in the custodye of the provostie courte : Therefore he shall paye the fyne of x*l* : which if he quyetlie paye or submyt hymself then to have the grace of the howse. To which assesment condiscended Mr John Blackall Maio' Wm Hurste John Blackaller Walter Staplegyll Robert Mydwynter and William Bucknam Aldermen of the saide Citie."

"XXVII March 1563. John Pyll was sent for before this Companye and being offered to be reasonablie used for the fyne assessed upon hym for the fardell of lynnen clothe which was staid and attached for the fyne of tenne pounds refused to conforme hym self to any order But with scoffinge and taunting required this fardell of Clothe to be redelivered with a recompence of xiij*s* iiij*d* for his charges."

XIII Maye 1563. Fine confirmed by the Mayor and Aldermen and if not paid he is to be apprehended and committed to the ' Warde of the Guldhalle '—

III.

"6 August 1563. At which daye Nicholas Martyn brought in for certen averege : viz., for the ' Angel ' of Dartmouth xij*s*, for the ' Julyan ' of Saint Malos xj*d*, for the ' Bartlemewe ' v*d*, for the ' Dragon ' ij*s*, for the same ' Dragon ' ij*s*, for a boote of Cornwall from Saint Malowes xx*d*, for the ' Mychaell ' iiij*s* iij*d*,

for the 'Charitie' vjs, for the 'Nicholas' of Plymouth iijs iiijd, for the 'Bartholomewe' vs, for the 'Mary Grace' of London iijs iiijd which amounteth in the whole to xxxvjs iiijd
"The 'Trynitie' of Dartmouth also paid ... xijd
and 'The Jesus' of Exmouth ... xijd"

Average money reported as received :—

			£	s.	d.
1563	...	...	3	7	3
1564	...	..	5	19	8
1565	..	...	6	10	11
1566	...	...	4	13	11
1567	...	...	1	15	2
1568	...	...	1	8	3
1569	...	...	3	6	3
1570	...	...	2	13	3
1571	...	...		Nil.	
1572	...	...	1	8	4
1573	...	...		Nil.	

1573 John Crosse to collect "averedge" money, and to have for his pains xijd of everie pounde.

In 1587 It was £17 10s (farmed out for this) the amount of levy being double—2d instead of 1d.

IV.

"The spirit of adventure does not appear to be confined to legitimate trading; for at the Court held on 9th September, 1568, it was agreed to take shares or lottes in the "Allottarie," and 64 members subscribed for 96 shares, " to be divided into three several posies," to be written in the name of the Company, and any advantage gained to be divided proportionately amongst the subscribers.

Nicholas Martyn, John Livermore, and Richarde Swete, are appointed to carry out the arrangements, and they bind themselves, their heirs and assigns, to faithfully perform their duties.

They chose respectively 32 numbers, running consecutively from 176916 to 177011.

The "posie" or motto of Nicholas Martyn savours of a spirit of pious faith :

> "Cast the Grapell over the boate
> If God will for the greate lotte."

That of John Livermore betokens somewhat of a hopeful turn of mind, and the absence of any pious aspiration, coupled with the fact that he was twice fined "for that he did spake onseemlie and unhonest wordes," may justify the inference that he was rather a loose fish. His motto is—

> "The Castell standing upon the whaves of the see
> We truste shall carrye some lottes awaye."

Richard Swete is evidently not a lucky man, but he knows how to take care of what he gets. His motto is—

> "If God doo sende any goode fortune at laste
> The lyons pawe will holde it faste."

In all three posies there is allusion to the arms of the Company, which were "A castell standinge in the poinet wave ij crownes in cheiff gold upon the helme on a torse gold and azure, A lyons paw gulz holding a grappell golde the cordes gulz mantelyd gulz Dobled argent."[1]

V.

"30 August 1571. And for that the accompte of John Pope threasorer in Anno 1569 by occasion of the sycknes in Exon, and the accompt of Thomas Martyn threasorer the laste yere, are not throughlie agreed upon and made perfect : Therefore it is determined that they shall bringe in their saide accomptes at the next Courte, which Courte is appointed (by Mr. Governo')

[1] From "City Guilds," a Paper read at the Devonshire Association Meeting of 1872.

to be one twysdaye the xjth of September next commynge, at nyne of the clocke in the forenone of the same daye."

[Minutes missing if any Court was held, the date of the next meeting recorded being January 1572.]

VI.

"20 August 1566. At which Courte the parties whose names do followe have ffreighted the 'mychaell' of Excester for lx ton accordinge to their complement as hereafter foloweth : To which they and every of theim standes bounden their executors and admynistrators to the Governo', Consulls, and Societie for the payment of their freight.

"The 'Michaell' of Excester to lade reesons
— Mr. William Hurste vi tone
   Thomas Martyn ij tone } viij tone

Mr. Morris Levermo' ij tone
John Hutchyns ij tone } vj tone
John Levermore ij tone

Mr. John Peter iij tone
John Pope iij tone
George Peryman ij tone } xj tone
Richard Mawdyt iij tone

Mr. John Mydwynter ... iiij tone

Robert Mywynter ij tone
William Chapell ij tone
Eustas Olyver vi tone } xiij tone
John Crosse iij tone

Symon Knyght vi tone
Robert Cotton i tone } viij tone
Andrewe Geare i tone

Robert Lambell } iij tone
Richarde Swete
Harry Ellacote ij tone } v ton

	William Perry	ij tone	
	Phillipp Yarde	ij tone	v tone
	Edward Lymet	i tone	
"The 'Bartlemewe' of Exmouth to lade reesons	Mr William Hurste	xi tone	
	Thomas Martyn	iiij tone	
	Andrew Geare	i tone	xx tone
	Mr. Robert Mydwynter	ii tone	
	Robert Cotton	ii tone	
	Mr. John Peter	iij tone	
	John Pope	iij tone	xii tone
	Richarde Mawdyt	iiij tone	
	George Perman	ij tone	
	Simon Knyght	vj tone	
	John Barstable	ij tone	xi tone
	William Chapell	j tone	
	John Levermore	ij tone	
	Robert Lambell	iij tone	
	Richard Swete		ix tone
	Richard Bevys	ij tone	
	Harry Ellacote	iiij tone	
	William Perry	ij tone	
	John Hutchyns	j tone	vi tone
	Phillipp Yarde	ij tone	
	Edwarde Lymett	j tone	
"The 'Mary Martyn' of Excester to lade ffygges	Mr. Morris Levermore	ij tone	
	John Hutchyns	j tone	vj tone
	John Levermore	iij tone	
	Mr. John Peter		…ij tone
	Eustas Olyver	ij tone	
	John Crosse	ij tone	vj tone
	Mr. Robt. Mydwynter	ij tone	
	Robert Lambell	ij tone	
	Harry Ellacot	ij tone	vj tone
	Robert Cotton	ij tone	

APPENDIX.   113

	Richard Mawdyt	ij tone	
	John Barstable	j tone	v tone
	William Perry	ij tone	
"Owners of the saide Barke	Mr. William Hurste	vj tone	
	Symon Knyght	v tone	xv tone
	Thomas Martyn	iiij tone	
"7th October 1566 The 'Christopher' of KyngesWeere: to lade secke	Mr. William Hurste	viij tone	x tone
	Richarde Mawdet	ij tone	
	Mr. John Peter.	iiij tone	
	John Pope	iiij tone	x tone
	Harry Parramore	ij tone	
	Symon Knyght	viij tone	xii tone
	John Barstable	iiij tone	
	Eustas Olyver	xij tone	xvi tone
	William Chapell	iiij tone	
	Phillipp Yarde	iiij tone	
	John Hutchyns	ij tone	xii tone
	William Perry	iij tone	
	Edwarde Lymet	iij tone	
"The 'Margaret Carwythen' of Kyngesweere to lade secke	Mr. William Hurste	xij tone	xv
	George Peryman	iij tone	
	Mr. John Peter	ij tone	
	John Pope	viij tone	xij tone
	the owner and Mr.	ij tone	
	Symon Knight	x tone	
	Richarde Bevys	ij tone	xiiij tone
	Harry Parramore	ij tone	
	Phillipp Yarde	viij tone	
	John Hutchyns	ij tone	xv tone
	Edwarde Lymet	iij tone	
	William Perry	ij tone	
	Robert Cotton	...iiij tone	

VII.

"Memorandu 25 August 1585. The Companie being assembled in the Merchauntes haule Mr. John Peryam o' newe Governo' elected did appere: And being moved to take his othe of Governor accerdinge to oure ordinaunces in that behalfe, answered that he woulde not take uppon hime to be Governo', nor take anie othe to prosecute the said office : for that as he alledged he did not minde to remayne in this Cittie as an inhabitant, but to dwell at London where his howsholde doth nowe remayne, and shewinge other cause that he must nedes be absent from this Cittie for the space of this yere or more, praied the Companie to ellecte some other in his stede : Whereuppon the generallitie acceptinge and allowinge of his excuse did dispense with him for this time, And thereuppon did order that ther shalbe chosen an other Governo' &c."

[Next day a rule was passed fining any member declining to be Governor, 20 marks.]

[In 1587. John Periam was again elected Governor, and he being absent, two of the Company were ordered to repair to him and require his direct answer, whether he will take the office or pay the fine.]

[17th August. At the next Court he took the oath upon "certaine condicons and protestations which were by hime then published and declared."]

VIII.

"1st June 1581. At this Courte Leonarde Thordon servant to Mr. William Hurst of Exeter Esquier : came in and requested to be made ffree of this Companye by redempcion, and the generallitie knowing that his saide master is no ffreeman of the

Companye, thought it not convenient that any his sarvantes shoulde be admitted. Yet not withstanding the Company weyinge the estate of the young man: at the last dyd agree by handes that he shoulde be admytted upon some reasonable fyne so they did put downe two prises, viz. iij*l* and v*l* which was put to be judged by handes. So the Companye dyd agree that hee shall paye for his saide ffreedome: v*l* to which the saide Leonarde woulde not agree. Yet neverthelesse hee had choisse and tyme geven hym untill Michaelmas next to respit upon the matter."

[Sworn a freeman on 16th October following, and fine reduced to £3.]

IX.

" 12 May 1591. It is ordered and agreed by the Governo', Consulls, and whole Companie that whereas Mr. William Martyn Maio' of the said Cittie hath disbursed for this Companie the some of three score poundes for and towards the charge bestowed in and about a certaine suyte for mittigatinge of certaine customes uppon wollen clothes, the said Companie doe agree that the said some of three score poundes shalbe repaeid him by xij*d* the clothe According to a certain agreement heretofore made by divers of the said Companie. And also shalbe allowed for the forbearinge of the said some after the rate of tenne poundes of the hundred. And that the said Mr. William Martin shall yearly at evrye yeares ende yeilde accompt to this Companie what hath been receaved, and that this whole Companie or the moste part of them shall passe sufficient assurance to the said William Martyn for answering of the said three score poundes, and the interest under the seale of this Companie to be paid in mann' and fourme aforesaid."

" 5 August 1591. At this it is ordered and enacted by the Governo', Consulls and whole Companie that whereas Mr. William Martyn Maio' of this Cittie hath disbursed the some of cccv*l* for and towardes the mittigatinge of customes uppon wollen clothes And whereas also the said Governo' and sundrye of this Companie assembled together agreed that a rate shoulde be set downe by Mr. Nicholas Martyn, Mr. John Davye, Walter Burroughs and Jasper Horssey for lendinge of a cv$l$ xiij$s$ iiij$d$ only for this Companie by sundrys of this Companie for and towardes the payment of the said some cv$l$ xiij$s$ iiij$d$ which rate being exhibited and brought in: it is therefore agreed that evrye persone and persons being rated as aforesaide shall paie suche some and somes of money as is uppon them rated and set downe within sixe daies next ensewinge, and that Mr. John Hackwill shall collecte the same within eight daies then next followinge. And evrye persone rated as aforesaid shalbe allowed of the said severall somes disbursed after the rate of xij$d$ the clothe that shalbe transported oute of the porte of Exon. And further the said Mr. William Martyn doth promis to satisfie evrye persone that hath disbursed the monyes ther severall somes within three yeares next ensewinge if the same be not allowed or paied in the meane seison And further it is agreed that the collectors of Exeter, Dartmouth, Tottenes, Lyme, and Barnstaple shalbe accomptable to the said Mr. William Martyn Maio' for suche monies as they shall receave, And that the Tresorer and Consulls of this Companie for the tyme beinge shall evrye halfe yeare receave accompt of the said Mr. William Martyn Maio' for suche monies as he shall receave of the Porte aforesaid, And to certifie the howse at the Courte followinge."

[Sixty-five members rated in various sums from £3 to 5s.]

" 14 Feb. 1593. Whereof an acte for a rate to be made amongst this Companie of a vi$l$ xiij$s$ iiij$d$ for and towards the payment of certaine monies disbursed by Mr. Willm Martyn in a certaine suite for mittigatinge of custome upon wollen clothes which saide suite was followed by o' Governo' Mr. Sampforde the saide Willm Martyn accordinge to the said acte did at this presente court exhibit his accompt to this Companie and in full discharge thereof paid to the Tresorer of this Companie a xvj$l$ ij$s$ vj$d$ with a iiij$l$ xs vj$d$ which the Tresorer had receaved of the said accompt wh is as muche as is restinge into certaine of the Companie which lente their monies. The rest was allowed unto them by xij$d$ the cloth at the Customе House. And by a taxacion which was made amongst this Companie for the full discharge of the said accompt. And so the said Willm Martyn by the consent of the whole Companie ys discharged of his promis made and agreed uppon in the saide Acte."

X.

"6 August 1597. Fforasmuch as John Martin inhabitante of the Citie of Exon and one of the Attornies of Her Maties Common Pleas hath well deserved of the Companie of Marchauntes within the saide Cittie tradinge ffraunce, in followinge there suite in lawe : And hath also made request to be admitted into their Societie and ffellowshippe, yt is therefore at this Courte enacted by the Governor Consulls and whole Companie of the Marchauntes aforesaide, that he the saide John Martin for and in consideracion of his peynes taken as aforesaide, as also for the good assistaunces that he will hereafter pforme unto the saide Companie in these like accons, shalbe admitted into the saide Society and ffelowshippe of the saide Marchauntes Adventurers without payment of anie ffine for the same, anie acte or actes heretofore to the contrarie notwithstandinge, Provided alwaies that the saide John Martyn neither shall nor will by virtue of his saide admissions use exercise or deale by himself or anie other in the trade of marchaundize, either directlie or indirectlie nor that anie sonne or servant of his shall nor will by vertue thereof claime anie freedom or priviledge in the said Companie. And therefore it is farther inacted by the said Governo' Consulls and Companie of Marchauntes aforesaide that he the sayd John Martin shall take an oath at the time of his admission in manner and forme followinge viz :—I do swere that I shalbe good and trewe to our Soveraigne ladie the Queenes highnes Elizabeth by the Grace of God Queene of Englande Ffraunce and Irlande defender of the ffaieth and to her heires and successors Kinges and Queenes of Englande. You shalbe obedient to the Governor and Consulls of this Companie of Marchauntes Adventurers tradinge Ffraunce. You shall

s

mainteine as much as in you shall lie all the libties of the same. Yf anie variaunce or controvercy shall at anie time happen to arrise betwene anie your brethren of this Companie you shall putt your helpinge hande for the pacifienge and aswaginge of the same. You shall not disclose the secreate talke commanded by the Governo' and Consulls or anie of them to be kepte secreate which maie be hurttful to the saide Companie. You shall enioy the libties and freedome of this Companie onelie accordinge to this presente Acte and not otherwise. You shall come to thellection of everie newe Governor and Consulls having no reasonable excuse to the contrarie. All and singuler the premisses you shall well and trulie observe and kepe so helpe you God."

XI.

"7th June 1571. Whereas the Governo', Consulls, and Societie have receaved commaundement from Mr. Maio' that the Company shall ppare as many men armor and furniture as they can, for the shewe of the watche on Mydsomer eve next: Therefore it is agreed at this Courte (holden the vijth of June) by the saide Governo', Consulls, and Societie. That all and every parson and parsons of this Company of Marchantes adventurers shall set forthe and provide as manie men armo' and furniture for the settinge forthe of the same watche as they can. And that they send the same men and furniture to my Lorde of Bedfordes place, by three of the clocke in the afternone of the same eve.

"At this Courte it is agreed by the Governo' and Consulls that the parties hereafter named shalbe attendant on Mydsomer eve next to take the vewe and be readye for the preparacion of the watche the same tyme: That is to saye—

| Harry Ellacote William Martyn } Consulls | To take a note howe many men, every one sendes in and to present theim to the Maio'. |

Richarde Swete
Thomas Chapell
John Davye
Richarde Bevys
Valentyn Toker
John Crosse
} to set theim forthe in order at my lorde of Bedfordes Place

Gylbert Cotton
John Maunder
Richarde Perye
Richarde Jordyn
Alexander Germyn
Davy Vylvayne
John Bugyns
John Ffelde
   Servant to Mr. Bruton
Ffraunces Toker
Richarde Dorchester
Thomas Chaffe
} To be Whysselers to goo with the watche and kepe theim in araye "

XII.

"18th July 1583. Ffor that this Companye have verie latelie receaved from Mr. Maio' a precepte that they shall set foirth certein calyvers armor and men for a muster or shewe to be synē before the Right honorable Lorde therle of Bedford at a mariage of the Ladye Elizabeth his daughter and the right honorable Lord therle of Bathe: for which cause this Courte being especiallie called: The Governo' Consulls and Companye have ordered and enacted that all suche parson and parsons ffree of this companye and others whose names are herafter mencioned: Shall provide so many calivers men and armoure as are to theim appointed and that the same be provided and made readie by the first daye of August next ensuynge upon payne that whosoever doo make defaulte therein, shall forfeict and paye to this Companye the some of x*s*., viz.

Mr. Michaell Gerwyn, Maio'	1 Calyver and 1 Corslett
Mr. Nicholas Martyn	iiij Calyvers, ij Corsletts
	ij almon ryvets."
74 members to supply	105 Calyvers
	34 Corsletts
	5 Almon ryvets

"And it is ordered that this Companye shall provide for everie Calyver 1 pounde of the best corne pouther that maye be gotten and hee that is the setter of hym fourth shall paye vj$d$. towards the same.

"And further it is ordered that Richard Dorchester and Edwarde Locke shall goo to the howses of all those which are set to their calyvers and armor to geve theim warning thereof and that they prepare and make readie the saide armor and men by the first daye of August next upon payment of xs."

XIII.

"11th August 1579. Item. It is ordered and agreed That John Sampforde shall receave in the wodd to be provided for the poore this yeare. And hee to have allowed hym ij$d$. for everie dozen. And hee to discharge one Gyll for his paynes or some other to helpe hym."

"15th April, 1585. Also it is agreed that Mr. Sampforde and Mr. Sweete shall have the woodhowse by the watergate for one yere viz. from the seconde of Maye next ensewinge in anno 1585 untill the seconde daie of Maye wch shalbe in anno 1856. And they do pmis to paie therefore unto this Company at thende of the said yeare for the rente thereof a vj$s$. viij$d$."

XIV.

"6th June 1574. Also it is agreed and enacted that there shalbe paid to the mariners at Topsham for wyndage, as it hath byn heretofore accustomed which is iiij$d$ to everie mariner. And also it is agreed that there shall not be hereafter allowed, nor paid, for any averedge dynner, above the some of xs."

XV.

" 15 August 1580. At this Courte it is ordeyned enacted and agreed by the Governor Consulls and whole Companye : that Mr. Philip Yarde, Governo' the last yeare, shall have xiij$s$ iiij$d$ for a Bucke which hee dyd provide for the dynner on the syxt daye of August last : And that everie Governo' hereafter that doo provide a Bucke to the saide dynner to be kept on the saide syxt daye of August shall have allowed hym also xiij$s$ iiij$d$ for same : over and besides his other allowance of ffyve markes."

XVI.

" 14 August 1578. Item it is further ordered and enacted by the Governor Consulls and Companye That everie yeare (one weeke before the syxt daye of August being the election daye) That the Treasorer for the yeare beinge shall paye and deliver unto the Governor for that yeare ffyve markes of lawfull money of Englande, to be bestowed by hym towardes a dynner on the election daye as before is mencioned.

" And it is also agreed that the saide Treasorer shall also then paye unto the Governo' vs to be bestowed towardes the Pot to be boyled for the poore prisoners in the Queenes Gayell, on the saide syxt daye of August everie yeare."

XVII.

" 1585, 10 July. ffor that the vjth daie of August being o' eleccon daie falleth this yeare on a ffridaie the Governo' moved the Companie to have there opinions whether it were best to kepe the dynner on the saide ffridaie or some other daie being a ffleshe daie. So the whole companie did agree to have the said dynner kept on the Mundaie then next following which shalbe the ixth daie of the said moneth of August."

" 3 August 1588. At this Courte Mr. Governo' did move the whole Companie concerninge certaine sermons and a generall fast that is appointed to be observed and kept at St. Peters o' Tuesday next being o' elleccion daie : It is therefore agreed by the whole Companie that no dynner shalbe kept in o' haule that daie. And that the money collected shalbe employed for and towardes the releiff of the poore."

XVIII.

" 31 July 1599. At this Courte Mr. Governo' did move the whole Company that whereas heretofore the dynner and thelleecon day hath been usually kept in the Merchauntes haule and for that our eleccon daie doth fall one a mundaie by reason whereof (Mr. Governo' beinge Maio') and havinge occasion to invite others as well as the Companie, It is therefore agreed by the consent of the whole Companie that the said dynner shalbe kepte in his owne howse."

XIX.

" 8 July 1596. At this Courte Mr. Governo' moved the Companie concerninge the dynner to be kept the vjth daie of August next being Ffridaie and a ffishe daie whereuppon the whole Companie agreed that there should be no dynner kept, and that the money allowed for that purpose shoulde be imployed in corne and geven to poore householders by the discreacon of Mr. Governo' and the Stewardes."

" 12th July 1596. Whereas at the laste Courte it was agreed by the Governo', Consulls and whole Companie that the money which heretofore hath on the elleccon daie ben bestowed on a dynner shoulde be bestowed in corne and geven to poore householders of this Cittie : It is at this present Courte by the

Governo' and Consulls referred to the whole Companie whether they shoulde paie there ordinarye quarterledge towardes the said dynner or dubbell towardes the releiffe of the poore: Whereuppon the whole Companie agreed that evric man shall dubble his quarterledge towardes the said dynner and releiffe of the poore and that the saide dynner shalbe kept the thursdaie before the elleccon daie at Mr. Governo' howse and shall have towardes his dynner the like porcon the last Governor had. And that viij*l* viij*s* vj*d* shalbe bestowed in corne and geven to poore householders of the Cittie by the discreacon of Mr. Governo' Jeffrey Waltham and John Chappell Junr., Consulls."

XX.

" 14 Jany 1572.—(14th Eliz.) And for that there hath byn of late contencion in brawlinge and ffyghtinge betwene some of this Companie which was presented at the Courte unto the Governo' and Consulls of this Societie: The saide Governo' and Consulls myndinge the quietnesse and brotherlie amytie of this saide whole Companie, and to avoyde and repell the like inconveynience: as farre as in theim lyes: The said Governo' Consulls and whole Companye doo fullie and throughlie agree condiscende and inacte (at this present Courte) That whatsoever hee be, being free of this Company, that doeth hereafter brawle with or geve any mysname, or other unsimlie or unhonest wordes to any other of his brethren, free of this Companye, that everie such parson shall pay to this Societie for suche his nastie wordes and ill behavio' iij*s* iiij*d*. And if any parson free of this Societie, doo fyght with or geve any stroke or blowe, or doo otherwise bodelie hurte any one of his brethern free of this Companye, that every suche parson shall paye to this Societie for suche his ill behavio' the some of vi*s* viij*d* or more accordinge to the facte, as it shalbe considered of by the saide Governor Consulls and Companie. And furthermore they doo enacte, establishe and ordeyne that whatsoever he be being free of this Societie that shalbe present or in companye at the tyme of such ill demeanure and misusinge of any parson or parsons as aforesaide and doo not present and reveile the same to the said Governo' and Consulls at the next Courte folowinge, That everie suche parson or parsons shall pay to this Companye for hys or their defaulte xij$d$.'

XXI.

"19th Dec. 1594. At this Courte it is presented that Nicola Owleborrowe, sonne of Clement Owleborrowe the 28th March 1594 did enter in the Custome house of Exon in the name of John Dorchester of London in the Pleasure of Topsham for St Malloes one ballett of kersaies conteyning xv yards twoo hampers conteyninge three dozen trymed ffeltes and three dozen untrymmed and one hamper conteyning seaven yards of fustain. Also the said Nicholas did enter in the name of the said John Dorchester in the said Barke called the Pleasure the xxxth of April 1594 from St. Malloes five ffardells of Vitteric canvas.

"Likewise the said Nicholas the 17th of Maie 1594 did enter in the said Custome book ffower endes and one small packett of kersaics conteyning xlij peces for St. Malloes in Brittaine in the said Bark called the Pleasure.

"Also the xvth of Julie 1594 the said Nicholas did enter in the said Custome howse in the name of the said John Dorchester from St. Malloes in the said Bark 12 ffardells of Vitteric canvas marked as in the margent."

"Also at this Courte Mr. Richard Dorchester thelder did confes that he did examyne the foresaid Nicholas Owleborrowe concerninge the foresaid eighteen ffardells of Vitteric canvas which he entered in his brother John Dorchester's name who answered that his said Brother was onlie owner of one ffardell and halfe of the said eighteen ffardells."

XXII.

"18th October 1564. And lykewyse the same daye John Ffelde was admitted to the ffreedom of this Companye gratis and freelie : As also was admitted to be Clerke of this Companye. And he to have yerlie for his ffee xiij$s.$ iiij$d.$ to be payed quarterlie : And lykewise he to have the makinge writinge and engrossing of all charterparties indentures of apprentisshode and obligacions of all the Companye. So that no privat nor particuler parson of this Companye do the same hymself : And he to receave for every charterpartie and every indenture of apprentishode ij$s.$ vjd. and for obligacion vj$d.$

"26th August 1583. And it is ordered at this Courte that oure Threasorer Mr. Smyth shall paye unto John Ffelde oure clerke vi$s.$ viij$d.$ for new writinge and enregestring of xxiiijtie leaves of this our common Courte booke into the greate lyger booke : which xxiiijtie leaves are last before writen and are not recorded in oure saide lyger booke."

"22nd August 1588. Likewise at the same Courte it is ordered and agreed by the Governo' Consulls and Companie that o' Clark shall have for enregistering of fiftie and odd leaves of the comon Courte booke into the ledger book a vj$s.$ viij$d.$ which is to be paid by o' Treasorer."

(He was present on election day 6th August 1585).

"10th Sept. 1586. At this Courte Julian Ffeilde's widdow did exhibit a supplication to the Governo' and Companie for xij$s.$ x$d.$ which her husbande was unpaid of his ffee before his death. And thereuppon order was taken by the Governo' and Companie that Mr. John Chappell o' Treasorer shoulde paie the same."

"3rd Aug. 1588. It is ordered that Julian, ffeildes widdowe shall have xx$s.$ in full and cleare discharge of all accons and demandes dewe to John Ffelde her late husbande decessed. As well by this Companie and the Spanishe Companie as by anie other waies or meanes whatsoever. And that Morrice Downe shall paie the said xx$s.$ for the use of xx$l.$ which the Companie hath lent hime for a yeare. And that uppon the payment of the

T

saide some of xxs. the saide Julian ſeilde shall seale a generall release to this Companie of all accons and demandes whatsoever."

"5th August 1588. And also it is agreed that o' Treasorer Mr. Howell shall paie unto Richard Collishett o' Clark xxvi*s* viij*d* in consideracon of the paines that he hath taken in wrettinge as well concerninge the treatie of peace betwene her Matie and the Kinge of Spaine as also concerninge Mr. Andrian Gilbtes voiage to China."

"11 September 1602. Also at this Courte it is agreed that Richard Collishett our Clarke shall have yearlie from hensforthe for his ffee fortie shillinges a sndhall in consideracon thereof inregister into the lidger booke all that is don the yeare before, and if anie shalbe lefte not registered the vjth daie of Auguste which is thende of the yeare he shall forfeite and loose his quarters wages, and shall write letters and copies of letters that shall concerne this Companie freelie without demaundinge any allowaunce or consideracon heretofore taken."

XXIII.

In the name of God Amen. I Henry Ellacott of the Cittie of Exon M'chaunt.

I geve and bequeath unto the Governo' Consulls and Companie of Marchauntes Adventurers in this Cittie tradinge ffraunce the some of ffortie poundes of good and lawfull money of Englande to be unto them paid in the Merchauntes Hall in Exon aforesaid for that tyme being at and uppon the sixth daie of August wch shall next ensewe my decease and death by my executors or administratours, the same to be imployed dysbursed and laide oute to thonlie uses and in suche manner and fourme onlie as hereafter foloweth. That is to wite: Ffirste I will devise and desire that there the said Governo' Consulls and Companie of M'chauntes Adventurers tradinge ffraunce till the same sixth daie of August in the M'chauntes hall in Exon for the tyme beinge deliver unto John Parr, John Ghere, Lawrence

Collibeare and Nicholas Strawe my servaunte the said some of ffortie poundes to eche of them tenne poundes, condicionally that evrye of them will then paie unto the said Governo' the sev'all somes of five shillinges for thust of evrie of the sev'all somes of tenne poundes for the first yeare. And likewise become bounden in sev'all obligacons eche of them comprisinge the some of twentie poundes with twoo sufficient suerties in evrie of the said obligacons to paie unto the Governo' Consulls and Companie of M'chauntes Adventurers in the Citie of Exon tradinge ffraunce, and to theire successors yearlie and in suche places as aforesaid and at and uppon the sixt daie of Auguste in everie yeare, the sev'all somes of five shillings for thust of everie of those tenne poundes for everie yeare during the space of ffower yeares then next ensewinge. And also at thende of ffower years next ensewinge suche tyme as they shall so receive the said sev'all somes of tenne poundes to repaie the said sev'all somes of tenne poundes to the Governo' Consulls and Companie of M'chauntes Adventurers for that tyme beinge and in suche places as is aforesaid. And in and uppon the sixth daie of August wch shalbe in the full ende of the saide ffower yeares. And farther my will and devise and heartie desire is, that the same sixth daie of August where on the said repayment shallbe so made, that the said some of ffortie poundes shalbe againe by equall porcons delivered unto fower other suche poore M'chaunte men of the saide Companie and Corporacon as to the said Governo' Consulls and Treasorer for that tyme beinge or to the greater number of them shalbe thought metest and best, then the said Governo' Consulls and Treasorer or the greater number of them then and there takinge of the said sev'all parsons, the like sev'all somes and like obligacons wth like condicons. And this order of payment and repayment to be so inviolately and truly kept and observed frome ffower yeares to ffower yeares forever accordinge to my intent and meaninge and not otherwise. And to thintent and purpose that this my will may be the better observed and kept I will and devise that the said sev'all somes of ffve shillinges wch yearlie doth amounte to the some of twentie shillinges shalbe by the Governo' of the said Companie or Corporacon for the tyme beinge be devided and distributed yearlie in and uppon the same daie in maner and fourme as hereafter followeth,

Two shillings thereof uppon the said Governo' three shillinges ffower pence thereof uppon the ffower Consulls and Treasorer of said Companie or Corporacon betwext them equally to be devided sixetene pence uppon the Clarke and Beadell of the said Companie betwixt them equally to be devided and thother thirttene shillinges ffower pence, residewe of the said some of twentie shillinges to be by the said Governo' yearlie paid unto the Mayo' of the Cittie for the tyme beinge and he to disburse the same againe uppon suche a pson or psons as by his appoinctment shall in the night seison give publique admonicon and warninge in the streates of this Cittie by voise and bell unto the howseholders and servauntes inhabitinge in the same, to be carefull of theire fiers and candelleight, According to a most prudent and carefull order of late begune and put in operacon and peaure (?) within this Citie of Exon for and towarde his and theire mainteunces and wages. Provided that if the Maio' do not bestowe this a xiij*s*. iiij*d*. for warninge of ffire and candelleight as is aforesaid : That then my will and intent is the poore howse of St. Anne Chappell in the Pshe of St. Sidwills without Eastgate shall have this a xiij*s*. iiij*d*. towardes theire maintennces for evermore."

XXIV.

"16 Jan. 1594. There was lre reade from Sir William Peryam Knyght Lo-Cheiff Baron concernninge the admission of William Prouze to the ffreedom of this Societie grate."

"22 Jany. Accordinge to my Lorde Cheiffe Barons request Willm Prouze is admitted to the liberties of this Companie for terme of his lief grate : and that his sonne servaunte nor apprentices shall not by reason of his said admission deryve anie priviledge or benefitt therby. But shall come in by some reasonable ffine as shalbe adiuged by this Companie hereafter."

"4 Jan. 1597. Also at this Courte there was a lre receaved from the Right Honorable the Erle of Essex directed to this Companie for the admission of John Prouse to the libties of this Societie uppon receipt whereof the Governo' moved the whole

Companie whether he sholdbe allowed a ffree brother of the same who were willing thereunto, and thereuppon the said John Prouse was sent for and in open Courte submitted himself for his ffine to the whole howse and for answeringe thereof hath putt in sureties viz Mr. Howell and Mr. Walker whereuppon consideracion was had what shouldbe abated him of the ffine of redempcion and in regard of the said Erle's letter it was agreed by handes that he should have abated of the saide ffine vj$l$ xiij$s$ iiij$d$ or in lew therof to provide duringe his lief a ffatt bucke for the Companies feast at thellecion of a new Governo' which bucke was offred by himself to this Companie, the choise thereof was left to himself to be answered at the next Court."

" 31 May 1597. At this Courte it is presented that Mr. John Prouse and Lauraunce Seldon did of late deliver verie unseemelie wordes one of thother in Northinghay, Therefore they and evrye of them shall paie accordinge to a certeine Act heretofore made iij$s$ iiij$d$."

" 22 July 1597. It is presented that Phillippe Prouse did of late deliver of this Companie at Topsham Kay these unseemelie wordes followinge viz that our Companie meaninge the Companie of Marchaunte Adventurers in the Cittie of Exon tradinge Ffraunce are a Companie of coseninge mates."

XXV.

" XIth daye of February 1580-1. At this Courte ther was a lre reade sente to this Companye from the Marchauntes of Totnes bearing date the vjth daye of Ffebruarye : the copie whereof doo hereafter ensue, viz.—

" To o' verie loving frenndes Mr. John Hutchyns : and the rest of the Marchaunte adventurers of the Cittie of Exeter.

" After oure verie hartie commendacions etc. Whereas ther growethe greate discommodities to Cities and townes corporate for that their are dyverse which use the trade of

Marchaundise and yet dwele not nether in Citie nor corporate towne dooth greate hynderaunce of the Corporacions through the whole realme whereuppon we have thought it convenient to write unto youe that if youe thinke it goode wee wilbe contente to deale by your advise in joyning with other Cities for the exhibiting of a bill at this presente parliament for the redress thereof if it maye be hade: That none shall use the trade of marchaundize but onelie suche as dwell in cities or townes corporate and if it please you to send any one man of speciall trust wee wilbe contente to sende a nother upon oure owne charges to solycet the same unto youre and oure burgyses by whose diligence possiblie redresse thereof maye be obteyned and further for that the greatest parte of the yarne of this Countie of Devon is imployed into fine kersaies some of them by meanes of fleas falslye made and bad wever are verie falslye wrought to the discredite and hynderaunce of the sale of kersaies which is the principulest commoditie of o' countrie and because the greatest parte of the saide kyrsais are solde in youre Citie and thereaboute where wee knowe youe feling the discommoditie of suche unlawfull ware doo thinke youe of oure myndes very willinge to have the same and any other suche disorder if possyblye maye be reformed. Lykewise wee doo most hartelie desire youe to showe us the ffrendshipp to let us have a coppie of your charter which is graunted unto youe for the trade of ffraunce wherein youe shall not onelie pleasure us but shall bynde us to doo the lyke if it lye in us. And thus referringe all thinges herein to youre consideracions and desiring your answere by this berer: Wee commyt youe to the tuicion of the holie ghost: ffrom Totnes the vjth of ffebucary, Youre lovinge frendes,

  John Wise John Martyn Christopher Savery
         Nicholas Ball Walter Bogyns
                Richarde Everie thelder
                Richarde Everie the younge
                Henrye Everie"

"Whereupon it was ordered that a lre shoulde be wreten to the said Marchauntes of Totnes certificng theim oure Companyes mynde herein. And that they shall have the coppie of the saide charter: paying o' Clerke for hys paynes for writinge it oute and also paying oure Companye xxx*s* which they are indebted unto theim towardes suche money and charges as they have layed oute and paied to Lytchefelde as tauchinge his late commission."

"10 Sept. 1585. At this Courte the matter was moved to the Companie by the Governo' to have ther opynyons touchinge a graunte from her Matie unto Sir Edward Stafforde Knight newe Lorde Imbassado' in ffraunce for the reformacion of karsaies. And the generalitie uppon the debatinge the matter did thinke it not conveynient to fall to anie agreement with the deputies of the said Sir Edward Stafforde touchinge the same, but to take respecte thereuppon and to take into the coppie of the comission to be vewed by some skilfull lawiers at the next sessions to have their advise and opinions therein, And then to geve answere to the said deputies what the Companie will do therein. And it is ordered that the said lawiers shalbe paied for theire paines by the Tresorer of this Companie.

"And further this Courte being contynewed in the afternoone there did appere John Cadye of Cliffordes Inne and Anthony Bickersteth gent : deputies and factors unto the said Sr Edward Stafforde Knight : And the matter being moved againe as touchinge the said graunte the said deputies demaunded answere what o' Companie would do therein. And forasmoche as owre Companie had not perused the said graunte nor had taken anie councell uppon the same requested some tyme to answere the matter, whereuppon the said deputies did geve libertie unto the said Maio' and the said Companye to take advise and respect thereuppon untill the seconde daie of November next ensewinge to give an answere unto the deputies at Mr. Glanfeildes chamber in Lyncolns Inne in London : What ende order or composicon the Companie will come unto concerninge the saide graunte : And in the meane tyme the said deputys did agree and gave ther wordes that they nor non other shoulde deale with anye Exeter men touchinge the said karsayes by vertue of the said graunte."

"And in consideracon of which libertie and respect geven : It is ordered that the said deputies shall have geven them by this Companie the some of a iij*l* vj*s*. viij*d*. which is to be paied them by the Tresorer of this Companie."

" Courte held xixth October 1585.

"Forasmuche as this Companie did promys Mr. John Cadye and Mr. Anthony Bickersteth gent deputies and facto' to the Right wo' Mr. Edward Stafforde knight to geve them answere on the seconde daie of November next (at Mr. Glanfeilde's chamber in Lyncolns Inne in London) what the Companye will do as touchinge the said Mr. Staffordes graunte for the reformacon of kersaies: which cause the Companye hath considered of and hath ordered that a lre shalbe written unto the said deputies to geve them to understande the Companys answere and mynde therein and that also Mr. Willm. Martyn nowe at his goinge to London whome the Companye have appointed for that purpose shall certifie the said deputies thereof on the seconde daie of November next which answere is this. That if by the said deputyes meanes there maye be a reformacon of karsaies had accordinge to the statute the Companie will be verie gladd thereof and do wish the said deputies to execute their office as touchinge the same."

" 1 Feb. 1592 : At the same Courte Mr. Governo' did move the whole Companie concerning an acte to be made at the next Parliament for redres in making of kersais for length and weight: Whereuppon the whole Companie agreed that Mr. Recorder and Mr. Peryam Burgesses for this Cittie shall prosecute the same. And that the charge of this Companie shalbe rated and set downe by the said Burgesses whereunto the whole Companie consented and agreed.

"And ffurther it is agree that lres shalbe sent to the Merchauntes of Tottenes Dartmouth and all other places adioyning to thende that one man be sent of purpose to the LL of her maties previe Counsell to thende that licence maie be had to trade to Morlais and Malloes in Brittanie."

" 15 April 1595. Also it is agreed that Mr. Henry Hull shalbe a suter for mittigatinge of excessive ffees of late taken for sealinge of kersies. And that uppon obtayning thereof this Companie agree that he shall have towardes his paines the some of tenne poundes to be levied by tenne pence the packe, and that he in obtayning thereof shall joyne with the Merchauntes and Clothiers of Tiverton."

XXVI.

"6 August 1589. At this Courte it is ordered that James Boyer for comitteinge of a murder uppon one hayman ys by the handes of the whole Companie dismissed and shall have no longer anie gowne."

XXVII.

"6th August 1582. At this Courte it is ordered and enacted by the Governor, Consulls, and generallitie, that the Threasorer of this Societie for the yeare folowing shall provide for this Companye three dozen of lether bucketts, two ladders and two crokes of iron for the helpe of myssfortune of ffier : which charges shalbe laied oute by our saide Threasorer and allowed upon his accompt."

XXVIII.

" 14 July 1586. Forasmuche as o' Companye do understande th' all such wares as was founde laden aborde o' Barkes in Morlis are arrested and carried awaie by the comaundement of the Governo' of Brittanie and o' men and marrinners are come home wee doe thinke it good that some good order be taken amongst us as well for the recovrye thereof, as also for bringinge of the trade to the Isles of Garnsey and Jarsey, and wee doe farther order that a Courte shalbe kept on Tuesdaie next beinge the xixth of this present and that lres shalbe wreten to the rest of the townes adioyninge that they sende two of there populace hither to ioyne with us for the furtheraunce thereof for that it conserneth them as well as o' selves.

XXIX.

"14 Feb. 1593. At this Courte it is agreed by the whole Companie that o' Governo' Mr. Sampforde shall ride to London and be a suter to the LL of Her Maties Previe Councell either for opening of the trade at Morlais and S. Malloes in Brittanie orels for bringing of the trade to the Isles of Garnsey and Jarsey. And that o' Tresorer Mr. Dorchester shall disburse fiftene poundes to Mr. Governo' oute of the boxe for and towardes the charges that shalbe disbursed in and aboute the saide suite. And a v/he is to redeme of Mr. Savery of Tottenes in London."

"And farther it is ordered and enacted by the Governo' Consulls and whole Companie that no person free of this Companie shall from the daie of the keepinge of this presente Courte untill the retorne of Mr. Governo' frome London with answere of the foresaid suit goo or sende anie wares or merchandizes to Morlais in Brittanie uppon paine that everye persone offendinge or doinge the contrarye shall forfeite and paie to this Companie ffortie poundes."

"3 July 1593. It is further agreed that o' Governo' Mr. Sampforde and Willm Martyn the yonger Merchaunte shall ride to London to procure (if it maie be) a ffree trade for St. Malloes in Brittanie and towardes the charges thereof Mr. Willm Spicer hath promised to disburse five poundes in money which money o' Tresorer hath promised to repaie the vith of August next. And likewise that Allyn Hackwills x/ shalbe delivered to Willm Martyn towardes his charges."

"19 Sept. 1593. At this Courte ther was an answere of a lre reade which came from the Merchauntes of Tottenes concerninge a trade to be brought to Morlais in Brittanie And that two sufficient persones should be sente to Morlais of purpose before anie trade be brought thither to conferr with the officers there As well for mittigatinge of excessive customes of late raised there As also to have assuraunce from them for restoringe of suche goodes and merchaundizes as shalbe brought thither: It is therefore concluded and agreed by the Governo', Consulls and whole Companie that no person nor persons free of this

Companie shall frome and after the kepinge of this presente Courte untill the laste daie of this instant moneth of September goe or sende anie wares or merchaundizes to Morlais aforesaid uppon paine that evrye person offendinge or doinge the contrary shall forfeite and paie to this Companie the some of one hundred poundes. And that Jasper Horssey shall fowrthwith ride to Tiverton, Taunton, Charde, and Lyme, and carry certaine lres and copies of lres with hime and take ther answeres concerninge the premises."

28th Sept. Time extended to 15th Nov.

"24th Nov. 1597. At this Courte there was a lre receaved from William Edney of Taunton touchinge the removinge the trade from Morlaies in Brittanie to Breste by reasone of some harde dealinge used to our merchauntes by the townesmen of Morlais. Whereuppon it is at this present Courte agreede that the said William Edney shall with all speede possible followe a sute for removinge the said trade from Morlais aforesaide to Breste to continewe for the space of two, three, or ffower yeares at the pleasure and good likinge of oure merchauntes and that John Marshall shall become debtor to the said William Edney for payment of ffive poundes to this Company towardes the charge thereof which some this Companie doe promis to repaie to the said Marshall imediately uppon effectinge thereof and that Mr. Jasper Horssey, Samuell Alford, Illarey Calley and John Lambell shalbe comitties for settinge downe in articles such iniuries and wronges as our marchauntes have receaved from the townsmen of Morlais which fforesaid some of ffive poundes is to be collected amongst this Companie by vid the ffardell homewardes from Breste."

"15 April 1595. At this Courte ther was a copie of a lre reade under the handes of seaven of the Lordes of Her Maties Previe Councell dated the last of Marche 1595 directed from them to one Thomas Edmonds Esquire now Agent for Her Matie with the ffrenche Kinge concerninge the mittigatinge of newe customes of late raised in Morlais in Brittanie upon wollen clothes: It is therefore thought good by the Governo' Consulls and whole Companie that a lre shalbe written forthwith to John Levermore the younger who beinge in London to ffollowe the said suite to the ffrenche Kinge for mittigatinge of the foresaid customes."

"8 May 1595. At this Courte there was a lre receaved frome six of the Lo : of her Maties Previe Councell (sealed) directed to Thomas Edmonds Esquire Agent for the Quens Matie with the ffrenche Kinge concerninge the mittigatinge of newe customes of late raised in Morlais in Brittanie : And whereas Phillippe Prouze is shortlie bounde for Roane in ffraunce, It is thought good by the Governo' Consulls and whole Companie that the said Philipp Prouze shall deliver the said lre unto the said Thomas Edmonds, and shall solicite and followe the contents of the said lre with effecte, and for his charges and paines he referreth himself unto the whole Companie who have promised at his retorne to geve hime that shalbe thought reasonable for his charges and paines."

"30 Nov. 1598. At this Courte Mr. Governo' did move the whole Companie touchinge a some of money to be collected amongest us towardes the procuringe of a clere discharge from the King of Ffraunce as well that noe letters of marke shoulde be from hensfourthe graunted by the said Kinge againste our Englishe merchauntes as also that if anie marchauntes shall hereafter happen to die within the domynion of the said Ffrenche Kinge that the goodes of him deceassed shoulde be restored againe to the executors or administrators of the partie deceassed without the contradixcon of the said Kinge, and that one pposer Newlande of Tottnes Marchaunte will take uppon him that the said discharge shalbe obteyned for ccc*l* whereof this westerne parte shalbe charged onelie with a thirde parte and the rest to be paide by London whereuppon the whole Companie agreed that John Marshall shall write to the said Newlande touchinge the saide discharge and that uppon his answere further order shalbe taken for a reasonable porcon to be paide by this Companie."

XXX.

"xix Oct. 1585. At this Courte the Companye do consider of the daungerous tyme that nowe is and howe it is like to be worse and worse dailie for the trade of us marchauntes. Therefore the Governo' did move the Companye to understande there mynd as what waies is left to take for the safegarde of o' shippinge and goodes : And at the last uppon muche debatinge of the matter the Companie did thinke it most conveynient that wee should be suters for an Jncorporacon to be had that the trade might be brought to the Isles of Garnsey and Jersey which the Companie do not doubte but to obtayne with small charge with the helpe and fartherance of the Right Wo Sir Ames Poulett and S' Thomas Leighton Knights Captaines of the saide Islandes : And forasmuche as the said matter is a generall cause and doo touche the merchauntes of other townes and places as well as the Companie do order that lres shalbe wreten to the merchauntes of Totnes, Taunton, Charde, and Lyme, to geve them to understande the Companies mynde and pretence herein. And that they call the merchauntes of their townes together to have conference about the same and sende us answere of their myndes herein with as muche speade as they maie and that if it please some of the merchauntes of anye towne to repaier hither on Fridaie the xxixth daie of this instant moneth of October next ensewinge A generall Courte then to be appointed for that purpose wee will be gladd to have their Councell and opynyons therein."

"29 Oct. 1585. There was a lre reade from the merchauntes of Charde as answere of o' lre of their opynyons touchinge an incorporacon to be sued for that the trade might be brought to Isles of Garnsey and Jarsey bearinge date the xxviijth daie of of October 1585."

"At this Courte (uppon a lre to the merchauntes of Totnes) Mr. John Hawkes and Richard Shapley did appere in their behalf who declared that the merchauntes of their towne woulde not agree that the trade should be reduced to the said Isles of Garnsey and Jarsey for divers causes which they do alledge yet not withstanding o' whole Companye did thinke it conveynient And did order that lres shoulde be written to Mr. John Periam and Mr. Willm Martyn nowe being at London that they be suters for the obtayninge of the same and for the orderly pennynge and perusinge of the said lres they have appointed Comitties whose names are hereunder subscribed, viz.—

Mr. Nicholas Martyn Maior   assistante
Mr. Thomas Bruarton   assistante
Mr. John Davye
Mr. Nicholas Spicer
    Thomas Spicer
    Richard Sweete
    Richard Dorchester.

XXXI.

"Memorandum that the laste daye of June 1578 ther was appointed to be raters for the levieng of (£100) upon the merchauntes of the Citie of Exeter and owners of Shippinge on the ryver ther: those fower persons whose names are hereafter writen that is to saye—

"Mr. Thomas Martyn
Mr. Phillipp Yarde
John Samforde
Richard Dorchester

Which cl is to be paied towardes the charge of one of the Queenes Shippes set forth for the apprehending of certen Rovers infesting the Costes of Devon and Cornwall.

"Me: That the one moytie of the said cl was remytted by order sent from the Counsell to the right ho. the erle of Bedforde."

"Whereat this Courte ther was a commission reade as touching shipping to be set forth at all tymes when neade shall require for the apprehension of pirattes that shall hereafter haunte upon these coastes. For answere whereof the Governor Consulls and Companye have appointed committies to debate and conferr about the same: those parsons whose names are hereunder writen: and they to bringe in their answer and procedings in writinge on Saturdaye next which shalbe the ixth day of this present that is to saye—

    Mr. William Martyn Governo'
    Mr. John Peter
    Mr. John Hutchins
    Mr. John Péryam

Mr. John Hoker
John Daw
Richard Swete
Thomas Spicer
John Toker
Richard Dorchester
Richard Bevys
Harry Hull

"Memorandum that the ixth daye of August 1578, The Committies last before named brought in their answere as touchinge the commission for pirates: which answer is hereafter writen.

"The answer to the Commission for Pirattes by the Marchauntes of the Citie of Exeter.

"In primis wee do moste humblie dutifullie and thankfullie receave and accept her Majesties most gracious commission in this behalf."

"Item for that to nominate and appointe any certen shippe by name for the apprehension of such Pirattes mentioned in her grace's commission may seeme inconvenient by reason of the saide shippe so nominated may be to farr of from the saide Pirattes or ells may be from home at such tymes or otherwise shall not be in good readines for that purpose; wee praye to be at libertie from tyme to tyme by vertue of the said commission, suche shippe may be appointed, and taken up in such yeares as shalbe neadefull and fyt for the same, as often as neade shall require.

"Item that suche as shall make complaynt of any losse by them susteyned or robberies done, shall deliver ther Maties Commissioners suretie or bande for the levienge, and defrayinge of the chardge of the settinge forth of any shippinge, for the apprehension of the said Pirattes, without charging any other inhabitant or other: to whom the same doth not apperteyne.

"Item if any such shippe set forth upon complaynte as aforesaide shall apprehende and bringe in any suche Piratte or Pirattes That then the charge of the settinge furth of the saide shipp may be borne upon the goodes of the said Pirattes onelie and not by the partie complaynaunte.

"Item that when any suche Pirate shalbe apprehended and brought in, and the partie complayninge shall there fynde any of his owne knowen goodes whereof hee is able to make sufficient proffe: we most humblie praye and request that the same Commissioners which shall have sett forth the said shipp for the takinge of the said Pirat may have authoritie to deliver to the complaynaunte his saide goodes presentlie without any further suyte to be made other to my Lo. Treasorer, the Chancello' or Barons of her Maties Courte of Excheker."

"Last day of March 1579.

"At this Courte all thes parsons whose names are above writen, dyd condissone and agree that the money collected towards the charge of the Queenes shipp of late sent downe for the apprehension of Pirattes shall remayne to the house to be imployed in wodd towards the relief of the poore, untle farther order be taken."

"14 June 1580. At this Courte John Weekes came in and demanded of this Companye certen money for his charges and travel which hee had byn at in ryding to London aboute the release of one of the Queene's shippes of late sente downe to this west coaste for the apprehencion of Pirattes: towardes which charges hee hath alreadie receaved liij*s* iiij*d*: and for that the Companye doo consider it is verie lytle yt is agreed by the Companye that the saide John Weekes shall have iiij markes more towardes his saide charges: which iiij markes it is ordered that Mr. John Peter shall paye hym owte of suche money as is in his handes of those that were rated towards the defraying of the saide charge."

XXXII.

"20 January 1590. At this Courte order is taken that there shalbe leuied of the Marchauntes of this Companie the some of fiftie poundes in money for and towardes the buying of one thousande weight of gonnepowder for her Maties better service and defence of this realme: Therefore it is ordered and enacted by the Governo', Consulls and whole Companie That thois persons whose names are hereunder written shall rate the whole Companie and certifie their severall names and contribucons before xxiij daie of Januarye next."

(24 Jan. 1590.—75 names put down for about £44, in various amounts from 50s. to 5s.)

"And furder it is ordered and agreed by the Governo' Consulls and whole Companie that on Tuesdaie next betwene the howers of eight and eleven in the foarenone of the same daie Mr. Michael Gerwyn, Mr. Blackall, Gilbert Smith and Walter Borrough shall sit in the hall for the receipt of the foresaide severall somes. And that everye person before rated shall bringe or sende unto them their severall somes and whosoever doth refuse so to do shall forfeite the double valewe of their severall taxacons And that the whole some collected shalbe left in the handes of Walter Borroughs untill further order be taken for the buyinge of the same powder And further it is ordered and enacted that evrye persone before named before the feast of S' Michaell tharcangell next shall have there whole money repaied againe. And whatsoever losse shalbe taken by the same powder shalbe borne by the Tresorer to be disbursed out of the Companies stocke. Provided that if it be spent in her Maties service then evrye man to stande to the losse thereof or to so muche thereof as shalbe spent."

"9th Oct. 1590. At this Courte order ys taken by the Governo' Consulls and whole Companie that whereas there ys disbursed by certaine of this Companie towards the buyinge of certaine powder and matches severall somes of money. It is therefore ordered that Richard Perrye shall have twoo barrells of the same powder at xij$d$ the pounde to be paid the xxvth daie of Marche next to o' Tresorer And that Mr. Nicholas Martyn shall have the matches for xx$s$ the hundred to be paid likewise to o' Tresorer, and also that o' Tresorer betwene this and St. Nicholas tide next shall sell the rest of the powder beinge barrells for the best benefitt and profitt of this Companie."

v

XXXIII.

"6 August 1601. At this Courte the Governo' did move the whole Companie touchinge c.c.c. weight of gonne powder to be provided for her Maties service. Whereunto the whole Companie did willinglie agree that there should be cccc weight provided, And that there shalbe a rate sett downe amongst this Companie what everye man shall disburse towardes the same in readie money."

XXXIV.

"16 March 1572. At this Courte at the commandment and request of Mr. Thomas Bruarton Maio' of this Citie the Governo' hath geven to understande and charged that all and everie parson and parsons free of this, that have any gooddes debtes shippinge money or other thinges arrested in any of the Kynge of Spayne his dominions, That they and everie of theim make their repaier to the Queenes Highnes Commissioners at the Guylhalde in London with convenient spede to geve them knowledge thereof (that restitution may be made of the same) Where the said Commissioners do mynde to set everye Saturdaye and Mondaye for that purpose."

"22 Dec. 1587. At this Courte there were divers lres retorned frome Totnes Dartmouth Lyme Charde Taunton and Tiverton together with sundrie noates from other places within this division of their severall losses and iniuries susteyned by the Kinge of Spaine and his subjectes, Whereuppon the whole Companie do agree that Mr. Thomas Spicer, Mr. Sampforde, Mr. Dorchester and Mr. Jasper Horssey shall forthwith drawe upp a a breiffe noate of all suche losses and iniuries as evrye the Merchauntes within this division have susteyned by the Kinge of Spaine and his subjectes and certifie the same accordingly, Together with a lre to Mr Wilforde President accordinge to the premisses which lres and noates were delivered to Mr. Sampforde by Mr. Governo' in open Courte."

"19 Jany. 1588. Ther was reade a lre dated the xxx daie of December last past directed to our Governo' from Mr. Wilforde President together with certaine articles concerninge the treatie of peace betwene her Matie and the Kinge of Spain. And thereuppon the whole Companie do agree that Mr Sampforde Mr Dorchester Mr Hackwell Mr Jasper Horssey Mr Bevis Pawle Trigge and Richard Wheaton shall with all speade conveynient sende into everye severall division a coppie of the foresaide lres and articles together with a lre directed to them accordinge to the said lres to thende that a perfecte note mought be certified upp for the answeringe thereof, And that messengers shalbe sent of purpose with the same And that they shall set downe some reasonable some for o' clarks paines taken therein."

"1 Feb. 1588. At this Courte it is ordered by the Governo' Consulls and Companie that the foresaid Comitties shall this present daie at one of the clocke in the afternone and likewise to morrow at the hower of one in the afternone set at o' haull and then and there shall take a perfecte noate of all suche losses iniuries and wronges as the Merchauntes of this Companie have susteyned by the Kinge of Spaine and his subjectes And farther that a lre shalbe directed to Mr. Wilforde, President, together with all suche noates as are already receaved from everye place within this division on Satterdaie next And that messengers shalbe sente to Topsham and Exmouth of purpose to geve notice to suche as have susteyned anie losses iniuries or wronges by the Kinge of Spaine and his subjectes to thende that certificates thereof might be made."

XXXV.

"19 Jan. 1588. At this Courte it is ordered that the Tresorer shall paie oute towardes the buriall of a poore Spaniarde the some of vs (if nede be) and the disposinge to be comitted to Mr. Watkins."

XXXVI.

"16 Dec. 1587. At this Courte a lre was reade directed frome the President and ffellowshippe of the Merchauntes Adventurers tradinge Spaine and Portingale dated the second daie of December 1587, concerning a certificate to be made by the Merchauntes of this division as well what losses they have susteyned by the Spaniards and Portingales as also what iniuries and wrongs they have receaved by the holy howst (as they term it) or otherwise Together with a coppie of a lre inclosed dated the xxvij daie of November 1587 under eight of the handes of her Maties Previe Councell to that effecte Whereuppon Mr. Governo' did move the whole Companie who shoulde deale therein which Companie did agree that Mr. Thomas Spicer, Mr. Sampforde, Mr. Dorchester, and Jasper Horsey shall send into everye division coppies of the foresaid lres and shall take a note of all suche losses and wronges as anie of the Companie have susteyned and to make certificates thereof at or on thisside the xxij daie of this instant moneth of Decemb and that in the meane tyme there shalbe a lre privately directed to Mr. Wilforde, President, conteyninge as well the receipt of his lres as also that wee have p'ceaded with as muche expedicon as wee maie And that the messengers shalbe sent expresly of purpose into evrye severall division and they to beare the charge thereof (if it maie be)."

XXXVII.

"3 August 1577. Whereas of late this Companye have receaved a lre from the President and assistaunce of Marchauntes tradinge Spayne and Portugall with a brief abstract of the lres patente graunted unto theim of late by the Queenes Highenes' as touchinge the same trade. All which were reade openlie at this Courte: And for that the contentes thereof are not to be answered but with good advise and deliberacion the whole matter is deferred untill the generall Courte to be kept the vjth daye next ensuinge of this present moneth of August."

"6 August 1577. General Courte.

"At which Courte the Governor Consulls and whole Company have chosen to ryde to London for theim to conferr with the President and Assistauntes of the Companye of Marchauntes tradinge Spayne and Portingale Mr. Simon Knight Mr. John Peryam."

(Simon Knight had "suche earnest busines" that he could not go and Nicholas Spicer was appointed in his stead.

A collection was made to defray expenses—each to contribute as directed by the Governor and Consulls.

Amount collected 10*l* 5*s* 4*d*.)

"12 August 1571. And it is further agreed that all those that doo disburse and lay out any money towardes the saide charges, and doo not enioye the benefiet and freedome of the Charter graunted to the saide President an ffellowshipp aforesaide That everie suche parson and parsons shall have repaied hym and theim backe ageyne by the Governo', Consulls, and Threasorer of this Companye all suche money, as they or any of theim, shall laye oute touchinge this matter."

XXXVIII.

"10 April 1600. At this Courte Mr. Governo' did cause to be reade in open Courte a copie of a letter and certeine orders under the handes of the right ho. the Lord Treasorer directed to the customers, and all others her Maties Officers within the severall counties of Devon, Dorset, and Cornewall for reformacon of divers abuses touchinge the entries in the custome howse."

"11th Sept. 1600. Likewise at this Courte there was a copie of a letter receaved from the Custome Howse directed to them from my lord Tresorer touchinge a newe custome to be raised uppon certeine kindes of cloths for fower yeares As by a rate uppon the saide letter maie appeare for revocacon of a certeine edict for English clothes in Ffraunce whereuppon the whole Companie did agree that there shalbe fourthwith letters sent to Tottenes, Barnestaple, and Plimouth and other Townes adioyninge to knowe whether they will joyne with us and become humble suters to the Ll. of her Maties most honorable privie councell not onelie for the easinge of the said rate but also to draw them to a shorter time or to take such farther order therein as shalbe thought conveynient And that Mr. Governo', Mr. Dorchester, Mr. Sampford, and Mr. Crossinge shall penne and peruse the said letters and to cause them to be sent awaie fourthwith."

"18 Sept. 1600. At this Courte it is agreed with the consent and agreement of divers Marchauntes of severall Townes adioyninge, viz., of Barnestaple, Tottenes, Plimouth, Tiverton, and Taunton that Mr. John Sampforde of Exeter and Mr. William Dare of Taunton shall fourthwith take instructon and become humble suters to my lorde Tresorer and the rest of the LLs of her Maties most honorable privie councell not onelie for the revocacon of a certeine edict for English Wollen clothes in Ffraunce but also to drawe them to a shorter time for the finishing thereof if it maie be obtayned whereuppon the whole Companie doe agree that Mr. Sampford and Mr. Dare shall have ech of them vl for and towardes there charges and expenses in solicitinge the said sute and likewise ech of them vl for there paines takinge in and about the suite which some of xx$l$ shalbe levied as foloweth :—viz., of Exeter vl xiij$s$ iiij$d$, of Tottenes iij$l$ vj$s$ viij$d$, of Barnestaple and the townes adioyninge xl$s$, of Plymouth and Tavistocke xl$s$, of Tiverton xl$s$, of Taunton xl$s$, of Chard xx$s$, and of Lyme Regis xx$s$."

"27 Sept. 1600. It is agreed that Mr. John Howell Maior Mr. William Spicer Governor Mr. Nicholas Spicer Mr. Richarde Dorchester and John Sandy shall fourthwith drawe and penne certeine articles for the better instructinge Mr. John Sampforde and Mr. William Dare in solicitinge the foresaid suite to my lo Treasorer and the rest of the LLs of her Maties most honorable privie Councell as well for the revocacon of the foresaid edict for English wollen clothes in ffraunce and letters of marke and Duncarkes.

"And also it is farther agreed that if Mr. Sampforde shall

disburse in and aboute the said suite more than the foresaid some of ffive poundes that then this Companie doe take uppon them to paie what he shall laie out over and above soe as yt doe not excede the some of three poundes."

"21 Oct. 1600. At this Courte Mr. Sampford brought in his accompt touchinge his charges and paines in ridinge to London concerninge the edict which did amounte to ix*l* vij*s* x*d* that is to saie for his charges and expenses iiij*l* vii*s* x*d* and for his paines v*l* which was allowed him by the consente of the whole Companie."

XXXIX.

"15 April 1595. Also at this Courte it is agreed that whereas there hath been for twoo yeares past an imposicon of a x*s* per tonne of Gascon wines towards the provision of her Maties howse and a iij*s* for wastage Mr. Mainwaring at his awne charge for the some of one hundred and fiftie poundes: doth offer to discharge the said imposicon: In consideracon thereof this Companie do agree that there shalbe disbursed amongst this Companie the some of a lxxv*l* shalbe levied and collected by a [afterwards increased to 10*s*] vj*s* viij*d* for everie tonne of wine that shalbe brought into this porte for this yeare followinge (if the said discharge be obteyned otherwise nothinge to be paid.")

"6 August 1595. Also at this Courte there was a lre reade directed frome my Lo. Treasurer for the clere discharge of tenne shillings of late imposed uppon evrie tonne of Gascon wines towardes the provision of her Maties howse which lre is to take effecte frome the xxixth daie of September next."

XL.

"8 Jany. 1596. Also whereas Mr. Willm Martyn Councello' before this Courte hath written and taken greate paines for this Companie touchinge the beatinge downe of excessive ffees heretofore paid to the Alneger. And whereas also o' Tresorer hath disbursed and paid to the said Willm Martyn a x*s* and to Mr Tickell a v*s* which is a slender recompence for hime consideringe his greate paines : It is therefore thought good by the whole Companie, that Mr. Governo' and the Treasorer shall content the said Mr. Martyn for his paines that shalbe by them thought reasonable."

"23 Sept. 1596. At this Courte it is agreed that Mr. Governo' Mr Willm Martyn sen Mr Walker Jasper Horssey and John Gandy shall conferr and agree with Mr. Newcombe Alneger what ffees shalbe paid from hensfourthe for sealinge of karsies and other clothes within this Cittie soe as they exceede not the price of xiiij*s* the packe and doe certifie theire proceedinges at the next Courte."

XLI.

"26 April 1586. At this Courte it is enacted and ordered that Thomas Spicer and Richard Sweete, John Weste of Tiverton and Richard Morgan of Collumpton shall accordinge to their discreacon for the ease and benefit of the Companie for the defence of Sir Walter Rawleigh and his officers And so for the takinge awaie of the excessive ffees uppon cocketes and certificates shall taxe and rate the whole Companie of Merchauntes as well of this Cittie as of Collompton and Tiverton : And the collectors of suche taxes shalbe John Applyn and Jasper Horsey which collectors shall not be taxed. And it is further agreed that the loane of all suche money which shalbe paid shalbe repaid to everie man out of the monyes which shalbe receaved by Mr. Willm. Martyn and Willm. Grenewoode which is xij*d* uppon everye pack of cloth which shalbe adventured by the Merchaunts of Exeter, Collompton, and Tiverton, And whosever shall refuse to paie the said xij*d* uppon everye pack shall for his refusal paie dubble, And the collectors to be allowed for theire paines xx*s*."

XLII.

"Mem. That the 28th daie of Maye 1586 the Companie beinge assembled in the haule it was ordered that Mr. Nicholas Spicer and Richard Bevis (either this daye or to-morrow) shall repaier to Sr Robte Dennys and request his wo' in the Companies behalfe to take the paines to sit upon the comission touchinge Sir Walter Rawleigh."

XLIII.

"Court held 13 June 1588. Mr. John Periam Mayor and Governor of this Company of Merchants assembled the said Companie and proposed unto them a letter articles and instrument receaved from Mr. Sanderson concerning a further proceeding to the North West Discovery. The Articles now dated at Mr. Customer Smythe's house the 18th day of March last and the said instrument was dated the 2nd daie of Aprill in the xxxth year of Her Majestie's raigne and tended to this purpose. That all the Companie of the said North West Discovery should put their handes and seales to the said Instrument constitutinge and ordynninge thereby eight persons viz Sir Francis Walsingham Sir Walter Rawleigh Mr Thomas Smith William Sanderson John Archer John Walter of London John Peryam of Exeter and Walter Buggins of Tottenes and any sixt five or fower of them whereof the saide Sir Francis to be and to enacte make lawes orders and constitutions for the orderinge and further proceedings of the said voyage as also to call to accompt anie of the Companie for anie matters concerninge the same and further to do and performe in all things as much as the said Companye mought or now maie do. Uppon the readings of the Articles and Instrument the most parte of the said Companie resiaunt here in Exeter there and then answered that they nor anie of them woulde consent thereunto nor put their handes and seales to the said instrument for divers and sundrie speciall causes then alleaged."

W

XLIV.

"6 March 1586. At this Courte it is agreed that all such psons as have disbursed and paid money towardes the bringinge in of the corne wch is by Mr. Willm. Martyn sent for and the money appointed to be paid unto hime that at the saefe arrivall of the corne the money shalbe by Mr. Nicholas Martyn Maior and Mr. Thomas Chappell paid unto evrye man so muche as he paid oute within twoo monthes after the arrivall of the said corne and John Sampforde and Walter Borough are appointed to receive the money and to paie it to Mr. Willm. Martyn."

"19th April 1586. At this Courte it is agreed and enacted that God sendinge the corne that evrye man wch have disbursed and paid oute there money shall have delivred unto them one boushell of wheate and one boushell of rye for evyre pounde by them paid out wch is to be disducted oute of theire some paid after the prise that the corne standeth."

"19 August 1596. Also at this Courte Mr. Governo' moved the whole Companie concerninge the excessive price of late raised upon corne and that corne was like to growe dearer rather than better cheape by mennes of the ffowle weather which hath ben of late and that he thought it fitt and conveynient that order might be taken for the providinge of some quantitie of ric from Danske or some other place for layenge the price whereunto the whole Companie assented and agreed that there shoulde be presentlie order taken for the providinge of one hundred tonnes of ric and that evrye person of this Companie shoulde sett downe under his owne hande what he woulde disburse towardes the buyenge of the same which rate was by them sett downe accordinglie and that everie man shoulde have the thirde part of that he shoulde disburse in rie and thother two partes to remaine in corne for the relieff of the poore and poore householders in this Cittie which two partes is to be repaied to everye person that disburse theire moneyes imediatlie uppon the sale of the saide corne And further at the same Courte Mr. John Sampforde was intreated to undertake the charge."

"20 August 1596. At this Courte it is agreed by the Governo' Consulls and whole Companie that whereas at the last Courte theire was a mocyon made concerninge the providinge of rie and the matter comitted to the direction of certaine comitties thereunto appointed sithens which time the Governo' and certeyne others of this companie have had conference with one Symon Leach of the said Cittie for the providinge of the said corne who came to this Courte and at the same theire was a conclusion made with him for providinge thereof who did take uppon him at his owne coste and charge to provide three thousand and six hundred bushells of rie good and marchantable to be delivered within the Barr of Exmouth accordinge to the accustomed measure in the said Citie of Exon at or on thisside the xvth daie of Maie next ensewinge at iiij$s$ vj$d$ for everie bushell and that uppon sight of anie bill or bills of exchaunge from the said Symon Leach this Companie is to disburse the some of two hundredd poundes uppon securitie from the said Symon Leach and one Henrie Gandie his brother-in-law, and the rest of the moneyes for the said rie to be paid in forme followinge viz thone moitie thereof within tenne daies after the arrivall of the said rie within the Barr of Exmouth and thother moitie within twentie daies then next followinge thadventure of the said rie to be borne by the said Symon Leach untill it come within the Barr of Exmouth and for performaunce thereof the said Companie have appointed and authorized our Governo' Mr Dorchester to passe the assurance thereof under the seale of this Company and to take securitie from the said Symon Leach."

XLV.

" 3 Feb. 1597. At this Courte Mr. Governor particulerlie moved the whole howse touchinge the payment of a certeine some of money which is to be disbursed for rie alreddy bought for the Citizens of this Cittie (which is daielie expected) whereuppon the whole Companie did condiscent and agree unto a certeine rate then in open Courte by them severally sett downe and that the said severall somes of money soe by them sett downe shall be disbursed and paid to our saide Governo' imediatlie uppon the arrivall of the said corne within the harbor of Exmouth allowinge to them such somes of money as they have alreddie disbursed towardes the buienge of the first corne and likewise that the same moneyes soe rated shall continewe lyable towardes the payment of the rie which is expected in Maie next and that evry man is to have thone moitie of that weh he shall disburse in corne and th'other moitie to remaine for the poore and poore housholders of this Cittie in the Garnett and that evry one that disbursed his moneyes shalbe repaied imediately uppon the sale of the said corne expected in Maie."

"3 Feb. 1597. The monies of such of this Companie as doe voluntarylie londe theire monies towardes the providinge of Corne for the provision of this Cittie with the sevrall somes by them graunted."

(£550—subscribed by 71 members—no amount against 6 names)—

3 "Widdowes" subscribed, viz:

Mrs Elizabeth Ellacott	... ...	v*l*
Mrs Applyn	... ...	iij*l*
Mrs Swete	... ...	iij*l*

" 10 Feb. 1697. It is agreed that Mr. Governo' shall nominate such persons of this Companie as shall attende at the Kay for the receipt and delivry of the rie theire and likewise for the delivry of the same rie into the Garnett in such manner as it was don at the cominge in of the last rie."

" 17 Feb. 1597. It is agreed that if the poore and poore housholders of this Cittie doe refuse to take the corne expected in Maie at the price of v*s* iiij*d* either at the Kaie or after it is putt in the Garnett that then evrye parson of this Companie are contented and agree to take th'one moitie of the said corne at the foresaid price accordinge to a former act and rate heretofore made."

" 19 May 1597. It is agreed that Mr. Governor shall nominate such persons of this Companie as shall attend at the kaie for the receipte and delivry of the rie theire and likewise for the receipte of the same rie into Garnett in such manner as it was don at the cominge of the last rie Also at this Courte it is likewise agreed that whereas of the last rie that came heither there was thirttene hundred bushells putt into the Garnett now it is concluded that there shalbe onelie eight hundred bushells putt in and that the overplus shalbe sold to poore artificers and howsholders of this Cittie that shall want corne."

"20 October 1597. At this Courte it was menconed by Mr. Governo' to this Companie that there might be a letter fourthwith written to Mr. John Periam and Mr. William Martin who nowe are at London to deal and goe through for a shippes ladinge of corne of a hundred tonnes or thereaboutes for as either of them doe not exceede in price vs vj$d$ the bushell at the moste to be delivered here But to get it if they maie better cheape and that the same corne shalbe delivered here betwene that and Candemas next."

"19 Nov. 1597. At this Courte there was a letter receaved from London from Mr. William (? Martin) as well touchinge the providinge of corne as also touchinge the confirminge of our charter whereuppon it is agreed by the Governo' Consulls and whole Companie that there shalbe fourthwith a lre written unto the said Mr. Martin to provide (if he maie) some quantitie of rie at the price of vs vj$d$ the bushell or less if possible he maie and also to certifie him that oure Companie are willinge that our charter shalbe confirmed at that, att Mr. Martin Councellors comminge downe there shalbe not onlie order taken for disbursinge of the charges but order for proceedinge therein And that the charter shalbe fourthwith sent to the said Mr. Martin which accordinglie was don."

XLVI.

"Moste humblie sheweth unto yo' Worshippes, youre daylie orator Phillipp Cane of the Citie of Exon That where yo' saide Orator is at this present in greate povertie, havinge a wyffe and syx children on his handes, and hath nothinge left for the mayntenInge of the same considers with hymself, that hee is not the firste that by misfortune hath fallen in decaye, and considers also that by labor, and paynes many have risen ageyne from povertie to a better state. Ys very willinge to take paynes to get his lyvinge and to bringe upp his children in the feare of God yf hee were able or had anythinge left wherewithall : And for that hee is one (as unworthie) of this Worshipfull Companye, moves hym the rather to shewe his grief unto yo' Worshippes, desiringe youe in the waye of Charitie to consider of his poore estate and to departe with hym some porcion towardes his releif, by some collection or otherwise as it shall please yo' worshippes, doubting not, but havinge yo' fartheraunce in the premises, hee, hys wyffe and poor children shall lyve the better ever hereafter : And shall daylie praye unto Almightie God, duringe their lyves for yo' worshippes in health and prosperitie longe to endure."

[32s collected.]

"6 August 1597. At this Courte there was a collecon made for this Companie for William Welch one of the Sergiantes at mace in Lyme which did amounte to xix*s* and for as much as the saide poore man's daughter did marrie with Arthur Jurden a ffreeman of this companie deceased who hath left three children behinde him the said Welch taking uppon him to discharge the Cittie of the keping and bringinge uppe of the said children It was therefore thought good by the whole Companie that the saide some of xix*s* shalbe made full xl*s* and that Mr. Tresorer shall disburse towardes the payment thereof a xxi*s*."

"10 April 1600. At this Courte iij*s* iiij*d* was given by order of Mr. Governo' and the Companie to a poore flleymmynge taken in the White Lion of Amsterdame by Englishmen."

XLVII.

"16 Decr. 1585.

"Memorandu—that this Courte was especially called for that there were verie lately certain Portingale Shippes taken by Barnard Drake Esquire and his companie sailing homewards from the Newfounde lande laden with ffishe which shippes being brought into the porte of Exon and Dartmouth the said shippes and goodes were taken from them and xxxviij of the Portingales sent to the Quens Goale of Exon by the Justices of the oute sheire where they do remayne in moste miserable case havinge nothinge lefte to helpe themselves withall. Therefore the Governo' did move the Companie to knowe their good wills what everye man will geve towardes their releiff. Whereuppon the Companie consideringe that it was a greete deede of charitie to helpe the saide poor men beinge in suche distres and not able to helpe themselves the said Governo' and Companie did geve towardes theire releiffe the some of   And also did order that o' Tresorer shoulde paie oute of o' boxe xxxviijs viij$d$ viz., unto John Sampforde and Willm Brayley for that they paid oute so muche money in charge to shippe and convey some divers of the said Portingales."

XLVIII.

"An acte for xl$s$ to be collected towardes the furnishinge of a walke under the Guildhalde."

" 8th Nov. 1593. Also at this Courte Mr. Governo' did move the whole Companie concerninge a texacon of xl$l$ to be levied amongest this Companie for and towarde the pavinge seelinge and buildinge of a certaine roome being under the Guilhalde of this Cittie whereunto the whole Companie agreed   And that Mr. Thomas Spicer Maior, John Hackwill, Willm Martyn Jun., Hugh Crossinge and John Tailo' shalbe raters and collectors of the said Companie for leviing of the said xl$l$ And that the same shalbe rated and collected within twelve daies next ensewinge."

" 16th Jan. 1594. It is agreed that Mr Thomas Spicer, Maior, and Mr Hull, Governo' shall take and receive into theire handes all the money already collected and that hereafter shalbe receaved and collected of the foresaid some of ffortie pounds which was geven by this Companie for and towardes the pavinge and seelinge of the foreparte of the Guilhalde   And that stones and winscott shalbe by them provided with conveynient speade to thende the same worke maie be the soner finished.

XLIX.

"2nd Nov. 1580 At this Courte there was a matter moved by Mr. Thomas Bruarton Maior of this Citie as touchinge a stipende to be paied yerelie to a precher: for to enstruct the youth of this Citie as well their Catechesme as also their dutie and obedience towardes God and their parentes: Whereupon it was ordered that a bill shoulde be made of all the ffreemens names of this Companye: to knowe what everic man would geve of his owne good will towardes the same. To which bill diverse hath subscribed with their owne handes what some they would geve yerelie to that use."

L.

"26 June 1599 And also at this Courte a mocion was made by the Governor to the Companie concerning a contribucion by them to be yielded for and towardes the restablishinge of the Catachisme and procuringe of a learned preacher within this Cittie the better to instruct the people in the knowledge of God which beinge thought a godlie and necessarie mocion the whole Companie most willinglie and freelie with a full consent did then and there agree ordeine and enact that there shoulde yearelie be contributed by the said Companie the some of tenne poundes to be quarterlie paid by the Treasorer of the same to such parson or parsons as shouldbe appointed by the Maior and Masters of the said Cittie wch are to nomynate the said preacher. And it is farther agreed and ordeyned at the said Courte for and towardes the payment of tenne poundes that from and after the sixth daie of Auguste there shalbe an incresse of averidge by a penny upon everic tonne packe and fardell, &c. &c."

LI.

" 15 July 1600 It is agreed that the Companie will give there seale unto the Cittie for payment of tenne poundes by the yeare towardes Mr. Snape's yearelie payment being appointed for a preacher duringe such time as the Chamber of our Cittie shall paie ffiftie poundes unto the said Mr. Snape and forasmuch as the said Companie could not agree how the said tenne poundes should be collected it is referred over untill the eleccon daie."

"6 August 1600 It is agreed that whereas at the last Courte there was an act made that Mr Snape shoulde have yearelie tenne poundes for and towardes his paynes to preach at certeine times in the week duringe suche time as the Chamber of the Cittie shall paie yearelic ffiftie pounds it is therefore fully agreed by the Governo' and Companie that there shalbe tenne poundes yearelie paid by the Treasurer of this Companie for the time beinge to the preacher of this Cittie to the use of such a preacher as shall be nominated by the Maio' and fower and twentie of the Common Councell of this Cittie or the most parte of them for ffive yeares or for so much of the said terme as the Chamber of the Cittie shall paie the said preacher."

"12 Sept. 1600. It is agreed that the yearlie pencin of tenne poundes which is to be paid to the precher shalbe for this yeare followinge paide oute of the common stocke of this Companie by the Treasorer the first payment to begin att Michaelmas next."

LII.

" 13 Oct. 1562. Peter Lake refusing to ' instructe and set forth in suche sorte as he is bounde to doo' his apprentice Richard Newman it is ordered that the said Richard shall be dismissed of his service, but in further consideration it was agreed that ' the said Peter shall enter in obligation of one hundreth markes to the Governor &c. to set furthe the said Richarde in a voyage to the parties beyond the seas on this side Easter next comming and that Eustace Olyver shall lykewise on the behalf of the said Richard Newman be bounde to answere the saide Peter Lake all such some and somes of money stocke or goodes as shalbe by the saide Peter commytted to the handes and truste of the said Richarde that therefore the said Richarde shall retorne to the saide his master's service and so to remayne with him in his service untill the ende of suche years as are yet remayning to come of his appenticehode, provided that the saide Eustace shall not stand to answere for any losse of the seas But onlie that the said Richarde shall trewlie answere his master in accounts.'"

LIII.

"13th March 1573. And for that order was taken at the last Courte by the Governo' Consulls and Company that Thomas Martyn, John Pope, William Martyn, and Richard Swete shoulde end certen controversies reveiled at the saide Courte, And forasmoche as the saide wardesmen have not ended the saide controversies accordinglie, therefore the saide Governo' hath taken a newe order at this Courte that the saide wardesmen, or three of them, shall ende the saide awarde atthisside the last day of this present moneth of Marche, orells everie of the saide wardes men to paye to this Company for his defaulcte therein xx*s.*"

LIV.

"To the Governor, Treasurer, and Consulls of the worshippfull Companye and ffellowshipp of Marchant Adventurers in the Citie of Exon and to everie of theim.

"These are to will and praye youe and in the Queen's Maties name, to require youe that youe call before youe all and everie the persons of yo' saide Companye and to straytlie charge and commande them and everie of them that they and all such as of whome the have the chardge or government, furthwith doo reform themselves in their and everie of their apparell of their bodies according to her highneses lawes and proclamations in that case late made and provided. And if you find any amongst youe not conformable thereunto to certifie us thereof that redresse therein accordingelie may be had thereof. Ffayle you not, ffrom the Guilhall this xth of Julie 1577.

  Robert Chaffe, Maio' of Exeter
  John Blackhaller
  William Chapell."

"At this Courte the Governor according to the Maior's precept called before him his whole Companye and gave them strayte chardge and commandment furthwithe to reform them selves in their apparell according to the Queen's lawes and proclamations in that case late made and provided and to cause all such as they have the charge and government of to doo the like And further willed and required them to kepe them selves out of daunger of the said statute and to use them selves in such decent order in their said apparell as they be not founde hereafter contemptious or obstinate in that behalf. But that they doo their obedient service to the good example of others."

LV.

"12 Nov. 1584 At this Courte do think it conveynient that Mr. Thomas Bruarton and Mr Richard Prowse, Burgesses of this Parliament for the Cittie of Exeter, shalbe suters that all Merchauntes and suche as be traders in merchandize beyond the seas which do dwell or inhabite in villages or uplandish townes shalbe brought to inhabite and dwell in Cities, Townes Corporate, market or Borrough townes, otherwise to desist from their tradinge and none to deal in merchandizes beyonde the seas unless they have benne usual traders thither for the space of xviii yeares past or have bene apprentice to some auncient merchaunt by the space of vij yeares at the least."

"And it is ordered that the reasonable charge of which suche laide out by the said Burgesses ys to be repaid unto them by this Companie within xv daies next after there retorne frome the said Parliament and that everye freeman of this Companie shalbe rated what he shall paie towardes the charge thereof by fower freemen of this Companie appointed by the generalitie for the indifferent ratinge of them whose names do follow, viz :—

Mr. Nicholas Martyn
Mr. Harry Ellacott
Thomas Walker
Richard Bevis."

LVI.

"27 Dec. 1591. At this Courte it is ordered and agreed that whereas it is supposed that sundrye Merchaunts of Taunton and and other places within this division have been suters to the LL of her maties previe councell for a licence to trade for Morlas : within the domynyon of the Kinge of Ffraunce, for staie and reformacon thereof the said Companie do agree that Mr. Hull shall ride to London and be a suter to the Councell for staie of the said licence and that there shalbe disbursed by o' Tresorer towardes the said charge the some of vj*l*. xiii*s*. iiij*d*. which shalbe collected amongst this Companie every man according to his liabilitie and the said Companie doo further agree that Mr. Thomas Spicer Mr. Richard Bevis and Mr. Thomas Walker shalbe raters and collectors of the said some of vi*l*. xiij*s*. iiij*d*. And to bringe in the same at or before the xiiij daie of January next ensewinge.

" Also at the same Courte Mr. Richard Hackwill of Tottenes

APPENDIX 161

beinge sent hither of purpose for staie of the said licence doth on the behalf of the Merchauntes of Tottenes take uppon him to paie the thirde parte of the charges that the said suit shall amounte unto and hath fourthwith disbursed towardes Mr. Hull's charges the some of iij*l* vi*s*. viii*d*. and doth promis to satisfie more if nede requier."

" 16 February 1592. Mr. Hull did exhibit an accompt of xx*l*. spente in and aboute the sute for staie of licences for Morlais whereof x*l*. is already paid us viz. vi*l*. xiij*s*. iiij*d*. by this Companie and iij*l*. vj*s*. viij*d*. by the Merchauntes of Tottenes. It is therefore agreed that Tiverton Cullompton Taunton Charde and Lyme shall paie of the said some of xx*l*. a vi*l*. xiij*s*. iiij*d*. this Companie other vi*l*. xiij*s*. iiij*d*. and a vi*l*. xiij*s*. iiij*d*. by the Merchauntes of Tottenes. And that lres shalbe sent of purpose to the places aforesaid for spedy payment thereof."

LVII.

" 8th Feb. 1593. At this Courte it was agreed that Augustine White of the Cittie of Exeter shall henceforth so longe as he shalbe of good behavio' remaine and be a common Brooker for dealinges in the trade of merchandize betwene this companie and anie other aliene stranger or anie persone or persones of the Isles of Garnsey or Jarsey and shall have and take for a prosecutinge thereof of the seller of anie goodes or merchandizes two pence of evrye pounde. And if anie other brother of this Companie have occacon to use hime in the like to paie penie for evrye pounde."

LVIII.

" 8 Nov. 1593. Also at this Courte Illarey Calley doth presente that one Robte Petter of this cittie feltmaker had brought home in the " Pleasure " of Topsham frome Pampoole in

Brittanie five or syxe yards of whitware not being free of this Companie."

(26th July 1594. Same man presented for bringing home in the Mary of Jarsey 14½ yards of "Tregar" which he bought at Pampoole.)

"25 July 1594. At this Courte it is presented and dulie approved that Robte Petter who nowe is and by the space of two yeres last past hath dwelt and inhabited within the citie of Exon hath divers and sundrie tymes heretofore adventured into the domynyon of the ffrenche kinge (not being free of this Companie and societie) contrary to the Quenes matie graunte made to this Companie in that behalf. And that he had brought home from Pampoole in Brittanie in a certaine Bark called the Pleasure of Topsham five yards of whitware and in one other Barke called the Marie of Jarsey fouretene yards and a half of whitware within one yeare last past the which nynetene yards and half of whitware were at this present Courte apprised and valewed by the oathes of Illarey Calley John Watkins and David Bagwill to the valewe of a lxxx*l*. whereuppon the Governo' and Consulls of this Companie with the advice and assistaunce of the roight Wo' Mr. Thomas Spicer Maio' of the said Cittie of Exon John Blackall Nicholas Martyn Michaell Germyn and George Smith now Aldermen of the said Cittie do seize taxe and impose uppon the said Robte Petter for his contempte and offence in adventuringe and transportinge the said nyntene and half yards of whitware the some of a xiij*l*. vj*s*. viij*d*. to be levied of the goodes and chattels of the said Robte Petter if there be so muche to be founde to satisfie the same within this Cittie of Exon or in default thereof his bodie to be imprisoned until he have satysfied the same the said some of a xiij*l*. vj*s*. viij*d*. to be disposed accordinge to the teno' effecte and trewe meaninge of her maties said graunte to this Companie."

(28 August,—reported that he submitted, and being a "verie poore" man the fine was reduced to 26*s*. 8*d*.)

LIX.

"6 August 1596. Also at this Courte Mr. Governo' moved the Companie concerninge a ballott of canvas which was taken as the goodes of one John Tucker and that a delivrance was served fourth of Mr. Maio' Courte by the said Tucker against John Watkins, whereuppon the whole Companye did agree that Mr. Governo' and the Consulls for the yeare followinge shall at Mr. Recorders commyne repaire unto him and take his opinion for answeringe the said playnte of delivrance."

"15 Sept. 1596. Whereas at a Courte holden the 9th daie of August last past it was ordeyned that the sute presented by one John Tucker against John Watkins concerninge a ballott of canvas stayed by this Company supposed to be the goodes of William Tucker and that it shouldbe defended by this Companie in presentinge the said accon in the Guilhalde of Exon. It was confessed and deposed by the saide Willyam Tucker and one James Bartram and his wief (the Jurie beinge sworne for triall of the same accon) that the said ballott of canvas with two others were bought at St. Malloes in Brittanie and brought home in a Barke called the Unitie of Topsham as his owne proper goodes and to his owne adventure, and that he solde the said three ballettes of canvas to his brother John Tucker for xxx$l$ before it was unladen out of the said Barke whereuppon at this present Courte the said three ballettes of canvas were apprised and valewed by the othes of Mr. Willyam Martin, sen., and Illary Calley to the valewe of thirtie poundes. Whereupon the Governo' and Consulls of this Companie with the advise and assistaunce of the Right Wo' Mr. John Chappell, Maio' of the saide Cittie, Mr. John Blackall, Mr. Nicholas Martin, and Mr. William Martin, nowe Alderman of the saide Cittie do sease tax and ympose upon the said Willyam Tucker for his contempte and offence in adventuringe and transportinge the said three ballettes of canvas the some of vl to be levied upon the goodes and chattels of the saide Willyam Tucker if there be soe much to be founde to satisffic the same within this Cittie of Exon, or in default thereof his bodie to be ymprisoned untill he have satisfied the same. The said some of vl to be disposed accordinge to the teno', effect, and trewe meaninge of her Maties said graunte made to this Companie."

"3 Feb. 1597. At this Courte it is agreed by the Governo' Consulls and whole Companie that Mr. Governo' shall with all speede conveynient write to London to Mr. Martin Councellor to procure proces against William Tucker for adventuringe into Ffraunce (not beinge free) contrarie to the Charter and that the lawe shalbe followed against him withall expidicon, and that the coste and charges in lawe shalbe borne by this Companie."

"12 April 1597. It was directed that Mr. William Martin Councello' shoulde followe the lawe against William Tucker for and uppon certaine broakes and contemptes offered to this Companie contrary to the tenor and effect of her maties lres patente unto them graunted and that the charges thereof should be disbursed by our Treasorer and whereas uppon the resolucon of her maties Attorney Generall this Companie is advised that the matter is to be followed in the Starr Chamber against the said William Tucker for a contempte in resistinge her maties graunte. In this present Courte it is now fullie concluded that proces shall this terme be served forthe of the said Courte of Starr Chamber and a bill there exhibited for the said contempte against the said William Tucker, and that the same shalbe by the said Mr. Martin prosecuted and that the coste thereof from time to time shalbe disbursed by the said Tresorer for the tyme beinge."

[31st Maie—W. Tucker came in and submitted, and prayed the Company to be good to him. He was fined £10.]

"3 August, 1599. The saide Governo' and assistantes did call before them Alexander Germyn, one of the sureties for William Tucker for payment of v*l* peell of x*l* dewe to this Companie the first of August last past, for a broake and other abuses offred to this Companie by the said Tucker as by ane act maie appeare and being demaunded whether he woulde paie the v*l* or not utterlie denied that he made any absolute promis for payment thereof, but that the promis he made was condicionallie that if the saide Tucker woulde scale him a bande for his discharge and not otherwise contrarie to his promis mencyoned in the said act, and so departed utterlie denienge the payment thereof wch matter is referred untill the next Courte."

"4 August 1599. The Governo' Consulls and assistauntes at this psent Courte did call before them Alexander Germyn and Robarte Parr sureties for William Tucker for payment of x*l* whereof v*l* was dewe the first of August last past and other v*l* wilbe due the xxvth of March next for a broake and other abuses offred to this Companie by the said Tucker as by an acte maie appeare, wch after divers and sundrie obiections by them alleaged yielded to paie the same according to the saide Actes."

LX.

"12 April 1597. At this Courte accordinge to an order sett downe in the last Courte Mr. Governo' moved this Societie whether they woulde admit Thomas Chaffe to the liberties of this Companie with the exception in his oath which he required which was not to be enjoyned to be a ffreeman of this Citie of Exon whereuppon the Societie did agree for sundrie good causes and reasons then alleaged that the generall acte in that behalfe before made not beinge contrarie or repugnant to the lawes of this Realme nor to the customes of this Cittie of Exon as they are perswaded shoulde not be broken, But that he shoulde willinglie be admitted to be free of this Companie takinge such oath as all other ffreemen of the same before him have don, whereuppon the Governo' of this Societie declared unto him the said Thomas Chaffe being present in the same Courte the resolucon of this Companie in that behalfe and offred him the said ffreedom in such sorte as all other ffreemen have receaved the same, which he utterlie refused and so departed displeased out of the same Courte having first showed the reason of his refusall to be this viz. that he had the collection of some fewe rentes dewe to the Deane and Chappter of the Cathedrall Church of St. Peters in Exeter by pattente for which he receaved an annual ffee of xx*s*. and therefore he saide he could not serve two masters, which allegacon this Companie thought to be ffryvolous and not to be applied for any cause of refusall of the said oath."

LXI.

"10 April 1600. Also at this same Courte it is agreed by the Governo' Consulls and whole Company that Mr. Sampforde shall fourthwith ride to Plymouth, Tettenes, and Dartmouth, to confer with the cheiffe marchantes there to thende that a suite might be followed to the LL of her Maties most honorable Privy Councell for reformacon of divers wronges offred by the Duncarkes to the marchantes of these westerne partes and that Mr. John Howell, Maio', Mr. William Martin, Governo', Mr. Walker, Mr. Dorchester, Mr. William Spicer, Mr. Burrow, Mr. Sampforde, Hugh Crossinge, and William Martin the younger, or six or ffive of them shalbe solicitors and followers of the said suite."

"30 May 1600 It is agreed that our Tresorer shall paie unto William Martyn the younger iiij*l* xix*s* ij*d* for and towardes his charges in solicitinge a suite to the LL of her Maties most honourable Privy Councell for beatinge the Duncarkes and men of warrs from our coaste and xx*s* x*d* for his travell and paines therein taken and to the Clarke for writinge about the same x*s*."

LXII.

"24 Feb. 1602. At this Courte it is agreed that lres shalbe sent fourthwith by a ffooteman to Tottenes Barnestaple Dartmouth Tiverton Taunton Lyme and Charde to this effecte to have theire opinions and consent that lres might be directed to the LEs of her maties most honorable Previe Councell for reformacon of divers wronges offered by the Dunkarkes to the Merchauntes of this westerne partes and also to have theire best opinions what course is fittest to be taken for the spedie reformacon thereof and to have there answeres here on Thursdaie the iiijth of Mche next by eight of the clock in the foarenone and that Mr. Dorchester Mr. Germyn Mr. Sampforde Mr. Hugh Crossinge John Sandye and Henry Sweete or ffower of them shall perne and peruse the said lres.

"And also it is agreed that John Sandye shall fourthwith ride to Plimouth to be a meanes to Captaine Turner Captaine of her maties shippe called the Antilloppe for clearinge of the coaste of certaine Dunkerkes now lieinge near aboute o' coaste. The charges of his jorney at this instante to be borne by this Companie and after by averidge. And that the said Mr. Sandye shall offer twentie or thirttie poundes to the said Captaine if he will undertake the wharfinge to be levied by pack and ffardell outewardes of the goodes laden aborde the "Pleasure" of Topsham or anie other Barke that shalbe wharfied by the said Captaine."

"4 March 1602. At this Courte it is agreed by the whole Companie as well with the consente and agreement of the Merchauntes of severall townes before named that one Merchaunte of Exeter one of Tottenes and one other of Taunton and another of Lyme shall fourthwith ride to London and exhibite a supplicon to the Quenes most excellent matie and to the LL of her maties most honorable Previe Councell for reformacon of divers losses iniuries and wronges of late receaved by the Duncarkes and Spaniardes uppon the Merchauntes of these westerne partes. And that everye man shall disburse the charges for this jorney to London and after repaied by averidge uppon pack tonne and ffardell. And that Mr. Governo' Mr. John Peryam Mr. John Howell Mr. Richard Dorchester Mr. Willm Spicer Mr John Prouse Mr. Alexander Germyn John Sampforde John Sandye and Henry Sweete and the said Merchauntes here present of the neighbor' townes adioyninge shall fourthwith drawe and penne certaine articles for the better instructinge of the parties before named."

"7 April 1602. At this Courte it is agreed that Mr. Dorchester shall have for his paines charges and expense in ridinge to London aboute the solicitinge of the peticon made to the LLs of her maties most honorable Previe Councell for reformacon of the iniuries and wronges of late done by the Dunkerkes and Spaniardes the some of twentie poundes which is to be levied uppon a vi*d*. packe tonne ffardell from hensfourthe outewardes and homewardes frome anie parte of the domynyon of the Kinge of Ffraunce and a vi*d*. uppon evrye tonne of salte and London wares and that the said averidge shall contynewe untill the some of one hundred poundes be levied and paid uppon the goodes and merchandizes which shalbe brought into the haven porte or creek of Exeter Barnestaple Dartmouth and Lyme."

"1st June 1602 At this Courte it is agreed by the Governo' Consulls and Companie that Peter Weaver shall have towards the furnishinge and setting fourth of the Katherine the some of thirtie poundes whereof he hath receaved in hand tenne poundes an thother twentie poundes is to be paid by o' Tresorer and whereas he hath receaved from o' Companie one barrell of gonne powder and some other furniture, the said Peter Weaver is to geve allowance backe again for the same And if he receave anie more powder or other furniture from this Companie he is to yeilde satisfacon for the same. And ffarther the whole Companie do agree that the gyfte already geven to Sr Robte Mauncell, knight, or anie gifte that shalbe hereafter given to anie of the captaines of her Maties shippes shalbe paid by o' Tresorer."

"6th July 1602 At this Courte it is agreed that whereas heretofore the lls of her Maties most honorable Previe Councell have ordered that two shippes of her Matie or a shippe and a pynnace shoulde be here to garde o' coaste ffom tyme to tyme during theist troubles and the same hath ben necligentlie performed by the Captaines of the same shippes. It is now ordered and agreed that Mr. Maio' Mr. John Howell Mr. Dorchester Mr. Germyn Mr. Hugh Crossinge Thomas Snowe Samuel Alforde and Henry Sweete shall conferr and take order withone Mr. Jopson Secretary to my lo Admirall that Mr. William Parker nowe Maio' of Plimouth and Captaine Sonds or some others fitt for that service maie be appointed Captaines of some one or more of her maties shippes that shall from hensfourthe garde o' Coast. And that they shall in regarde of the good will and frendshippe of the said Mr. Jopson geve him twentie poundes or a greater some if the said Comitties shall thinke fitt. And that the said Comitties shall drawe and penne lres to be directed to the neighbor' townes adioyninge as well to the owners of shippinge as to the Merchauntes there not onelie to be contributorie towardes the said charge, but also to joyne in [mutilated]."

LXIII.

"26 June 1599. At this Courte William Newcombe of this Cittie Draper made request to this Companie to be admitted a ffreeman of the same and for his ffine he referred himself to the whole howse thereuppon it was agreed by the said Companie that he shoulde be admitted a ffreeman for the ffine of twentie markes accordinge to a certaine former act in that behalf provided and soe did putt in sureties for answeringe thereof to the Tresorer the first of August next viz. Alexander Germyn and John Sandye. Nevertheless the said William Newcombe made humble suite to have mittigacon of parte of the said ffine. In consideracon whereof and speciallie in regarde of a verie favorable letter written by Mr. Leach, preacher, and one of the Cannons of Exeter written to the Governor in that behalf in favor of the said William Newcombe it was condiscended and agreed there shoulde be ffive markes abated of the saide ffine abovemenconed and for the said William Newcombe should paie onlie x/. for his said ffreedom to the said Tresorer at the daye aforesaid."

MISCELLANEA.

Examples of Minutes.

"15 May 1562. At which daye also John Cotton brought his indentures into this Courte and thereby it appered he was bounde for seven yeares as an apprentise to Robert Cotton his ffather, which he hath faithfullie served, as appereth by proffe: wherefore he is admytted to the freedome of this Companye grates: payinge onlie the ffees of the Courte."

"23 August, 1569. Item at this Courte yt was agreed and thought good by the Governo' Consulls and Companye that the awarde next hereafter writen shoulde regestred and recorded in this booke ffor that the contentes and paymentes in the saide awarde mencioned are not performed nor kepte of the partie of William Parsons : who dyd receve and accept, at the handes of the umpiers hereunder named the lyke counterpane of the saide awarde : Sealed with the severall seales of the said umpiers and signed with their handes : And further order is taken that the Clarke of this Companye shall have for his paines for the recording of this awarde and for every one that shalbe hereafter recorded in this booke :

The Awarde.

." Thes presentes made the seconde daye of Aprill in the tenth yere of the reigne of oure sovereigne Ladye Elizabeth by the grace of God Queene of Englande Ffraunce and Irelande Defendo' of the faith &c. &c. Witnesseth that where there is certen matters in controversie and now hanging and depending at the lawe betwene Mychaell German and William Parsons of the Citie of Excester Marchauntes : And where at a Courte of the Companye of Marchant Adventurers of the saide Citie of Excester holden and kept the xxvi of ffebruary last past : the saide matters in controversie were revealed at the saide Courte, and then and there at that present it was ordered condiscended and agreed by the said Mychaell German and William Parsons that Eustas Olyver, Nicholas Martyn, Robert Lambell and John Hutchyns of the said Citie Marchantes should have the hyriage of all such matters in controversie betwene theim : And that they should be their Arbitrators in that behalf : And it was then further condiscended concluded and agreed by the saide Mychaell German and William Parsons.

" That yf the saide Wardesmen dyd not fynish their awarde by a daye then lymited (indifferently accordinge to the judgement of both parties) That then the said Michael German and William shoulde abide the fynal ende determinacon and judgement in that behalf, of two umpires then also indifferently chosen by and betwene the saide parties That is to saye Thomas Prestwood and John Pope of the saide Citie Marchauntes And for that the saide Wardesmen have fynished their awarde and not to the full contentacon of bothe the saide parties Therefore wee the saide umpires doo make ordeyne determyne and yealde upp this oure fynall ende, as touching the premisses in maner and form following : ffyrst we the said umpires doo throughlie conclude and ffynish That William Parsons his executor or assignes in discharge of all debtes and demaundes shall paye or cause to be paide to the above named Mychaell German his executors or assignes the some of ffyftie poundes and three shillinges of lawful money of Englande in maner and forme folowinge That is to wete in the seconde daye of August next ensuying xvj*l* xiij*s* iiij*d* and in the seconde daye of November then next ensuing other xvj*l* xiij*s* iiij*d* and in the seconde daye of Ffebruary then next followinge xvj*l* xiij*s* iiij*d* in full contentacon and payment of the saide some of ffyftie poundes and three shillinges : and for the performance thereof wee the said umpires doo conclude and agree that the saide William Parsons at the yealding upp of this oure fynall ende shall put into the handes of the saide Mychaell German and his assignes a sufficient paune and assurance for the trewe payment and answeringe of the saide some of ffyftie poundes and three shillings to the saide Mychaell German or his assignes in maner and forme aforesaid And further wee doo conclude and determyne that the abovesaide Mychaell German or his assignes shall paye to Valentine Toker for Alexander German apprentice unto the saide William Parsons for his being in Roane the money which the said Valentyne Toker dyd dysburse and laye oute in Roane to the charges and tabels of the saide Alexander in learning his language To be paide to the same Valentyne or his assignes in the xvith daye next comminge of this present moneth of April And further also we doo conclude, agree and determyne, That William Parsons shall yealde and release the apprentishipp of his apprentise Alexander German with his indenture and all other right claymes which he nowe hath or ought to have of hym by or for his servyse or otherwyse. Shall clerelie deliver him to his saide ffather with all his apparell that was made for hym which unto hym apperteyneth (whereof wee have had consideracions) we saye to deliver him to his saide ffather Mychael German in the xvith daye next ensuying of this present moneth of Aprill without any delaye or let whatsoever: In witness whereof wee the said Umpiers have to thes presentes severallie put o' handes and scales: the daye and yeare above written."

Apprentices.

"No man free of this Companye shall after the daye of the kepinge of this presente Courte: that is to say after this presente thyrde day of Ffebruary 1578 take any apprentice to be bounde for any lesse term then eight yeares, nor the yeares of any such apprentise shall ende before he be of age of ffower and twentie yeares upon paine of ten poundes. Provided alwaies that if any apprentise have served any part of his yeares (being bounde as above specified) with any brother of this Companye: That then such yeares shalbe allowed yf he serve oute the residue of his terme with any other ffreeman of this Companyé."

"21 Nov. 1587. Mr. Governo' did move the Companie cerninge a fyne to be paid by evrye apprentice that hereafter shalbe licensed to deale by himselfe in the pties beyonde the seas who agreed that a fine shoulde be paid. Whereupon Mr. Governo' did set downe two prises vizt. xs and vi$s$ viij$d$. And thereupon the whole Companie did agree uppon vi$s$ viij$d$. And that the Clarke shall have for entering thereof a vj$d$ and the Beadell for his ffee a iiij$d$ over and besides the said some of a a vj$s$ viij$d$. And beinge so admitted shalbe sufficiently licenced to trade for himselfe anie former acte notwithstandinge."

"14 Feb. 1593. At this Courte John Cuppwill Apprentice to Walter Horssey is licenced to trade for himselfe in the ptes beyonde the seas anie acte heretofore made to the contrarye notwithstandinge: and paid the ffee to Mr. Tresorer videlt a vj$s$ viij$d$."

"26 June 1595. Alexander Maurice Apprentice to Mr. Bevis came in and took the oathe of a freeman as an apprentice within his terme and paid the ffees of the Courte viz., vs."

"26 June 1595. Also at this Courte Henry Austine late apprentice to Mr. John Davie Maior, came in and praied this Companie to be allowed a Ffreeman And for as muche as the said Henry did not come into this Courte and praie this Companie to be allowed a ffreeman within a yeare after thende of his terme accordinge to a certaine Acte heretofore made, Therefore he shall paie to this Companie the some of a x*l*. accordinge to the saide Acte : Whereuppon the saide Henry Austine did referr himself for the said ffine to the whole house and hath put in for sureties for answeringe thereof viz. Mr. Dorchester th'elder and Walter Burrows whereuppon the whole Companie agreed that he shoulde have abated of the saide some of a x*l* eight poundes and so he is to paie to o' Treasorer ffortie shillinges And thereuppon allowed a ffreeman."

"1st Sept. 1580. At this Courte William Yarde the eldest sone of Mr. Phillipp Yarde came in and claymed the freedome of this Companye by patrimonye and according to o' actes and ordynaunces hee was allowed."

Fines for Offences.

"15 May 1562. Whereas Nicholas Eron Baker hathe confessed in open Courte that he hathe traffiqued from Saint Mallowes in the parties of Brytayne unto this Citie certen lynnen clothe contrarye to the Charter. That therefore he shall paye for the saide offence the some of vi*s*. viii*d*."

"23 Sept. 1562. At which daye it was ordeyned and determyned that forasmuche as John Peryam Marchant hath from tyme to tyme traffiqued out of this realme into the parties of Ffraunce and other the dominions of the Ffrenche Kinge and lykewise hath traffiqued his wares and m'chandise from out of the domynions of the Ffrench Kinge into this realme of England as namelie xxx peces of cresse laden in the Marye Page in the moneth of   last : Yt is therefore ordered by the Governo' Consulls and Co'panye with the assistance and advyse of Mr. William Hurste Maio' Mr. John Mydwynter, Mr. William Bucknam, Mr. John Peter and Mr. Robert Mydwynter Aldermen That the said John Peryam shall paye for his fyne for his foresaide traffiques contrarye to thorder and tenure of the Charter of this Companye the some of xxtie markes.

"6 Aug. 1571. General Court "At which Courte it is ordeyned enacted and agreed by the Governo' Consulls and whole Companye, that if any parson of this Societie doo presume, and do come into the Courte without his gowne at the election of a newe Governo' being the syxth daye of Auguste : that every suche parson shall paye for his defaulte xij*d*. every younge man that is not maryed and hath no gowne onlie excepted."

26 Feb. 1582. An Act passed assessing fines for adventuring (not being free of the Company) at 3*s* 4*d* in the pound on the value of the goods.

6 Sept. 1592. Edward Chicke fined 16*l* 13*s*. 4*d*. afterwards reduced on submission to 10*l* and William Angevyn 20*l* "or in defaulte thereof his bodie to be imprisoned."

"14 Feb. 1593. Willm. Gill for bringing home two peces and a quarter of Dowlis in the 'Diana' of Lyme 40*s*."

26 June 1595. Thomas Pope fined 3*s*. 4*d*. for leaving the dinner table without leave.

31 May 1597. William Ffice for adventuring with "Devonsheere karseyes" and John Ffice with "three buttes of sacke from St. Malloes."

For Admission to the Guild.

		£	s.	d.
26 May 1562.	Thomas Chappell	1	10	0
13 May 1573.	George Smith	6	13	4
,,	Gilbert Staplegill		10	0
,,	John Dallet		6	8
,,	Thomas Bogyns		3	4
16 June 1576.	Thomas Richardson	1	0	0
2 Nov. 1580.	Richard Colthurst	2	0	0
4 May 1581.	Nicholas Shevilier a Jerseyman	5	0	0
,,	John Younge (considering his poor estate)	2	0	0
3 July 1593.	Allyn Hackwill	2	0	0
,,	John Lante	8	0	0

"8 May 1595. John Wilmouth a mere Merchant on delivering to the Treasore one Ilande spruse cloth of the valewe of three poundes—in length eight spannes and in breadeth ffower spannes."

Unpaid Debts.

"6 August 1562. Which have wholie agreed that Harrie Maunder who is debitor to the Companye for xxij*s* vij*d* and Richarde Hockleighe debitor for iij*l* and Hubert Colwell for xxiij*s* iiij*d* and Mr. Richarde Prestwodde for liiij*s* viij*d* And every of them shall furthwith paye their severall debtes dewe: Orelles put in Sureties, or remayne in warde untill payment be be made."

"6 August 1565. Yt is agreed that what soever he be being indetted to the Companye having warning to bringe in and paye the same debte at the Courte at a certen daye and tyme appointed: Yf he do not bringe in and paye suche some and somes of money in manner aforesaide, That then everye suche parson so offending to pay the saide debte and to paie two pence over and besides upon every shilling of the same some."

"1 Sept. 1580. That all suche parsons free of this Companye which doo refuse or doo not paye their dutie due to the howse and by meanes thereof, the same as set downe and writen in the Blacke Booke that everie such parson shall paye to this Companie for his defaulet therein: Doble the value thereof: without any remission or pardon."

House Money.

"15 April 1585. To have the stock of the house for the year—20*l*—Morrice Downe, in consequence of his great loss at sea by Rovers."

"24 Augst. 1592. Lent to Elizbth. Webber, widdowe."

"28 Augst. 1593. Lent to Mr. Sampforde in consequence of his great losses by sea."

"20 Augst. 1601. To Andrew Geare."

Charge for Seal.

"16 Dec. 1568. It is concluded and agreed by the Governo' &c., That whosoever he bee that shall have the seale of this Companye to any writing shall paye therfore to the use of this Societie ijs."

Accounts.

"7 Oct. 1561. Nicholas Marten answered for iiij avereges whereof three were for Flaunders and one for Biskaye."

"26 October 1563. Order was taken. That Richarde Prestwodde Eustace Olyver Edwarde Lymet and Symon Knyght shall have the perusall of all the accomptes as well of the credytt as of the debtes of this Companye and to geve the trewe reporte thereof that the debtes of the Companye may be dischargedd. Every of theim making defaulct to paye xs."

"18 Dec. 1599. It is agreed by the Governor Consulls and whole Companie that there shalbe a rate sett downe by this Companie for the payment of tenne pounds towardes the charge of Mr. Coombe solicitinge a suite to the LL of her maties honorable Previe Councell for avoidinge of certaine orders and decrees of late raised and sett downe in Rochell whereuppon the whole Companie did agree that the some of tenne poundes shalbe levied as followeth viz. of Exeter iij$l$ vi$s$ viij$d$ of Totnes iij$l$ vj$d$ viij$s$ of Barnestaple xxxiij$s$ iiij$d$ and of Tiverton xxxiij$s$ iiij$d$ and that the some of tenne poundes shalbe levied in Rochell by two sufficient English Marchauntes there after the rate of xiij$d$ the packe and soe after that rate uppon all other marchaundizes that shoulde be brought thither."

Exclusive Trading.

"26 June 1600. At this Courte there was a coppie of a letter reade directed to Sir Thomas Ridgwaie Knight from Richard Carmarden Esquier touchinge a trade to the Levaunt seas together with a copie of an answere from the Marchauntes of Bristoll to the saide Richard Carmarden concerninge the said trade. Whereuppon Mr. Governor did move the whole Companie howe many of them would yielde and agree to be free and trade thether. And thereuppon those parsons whose names are subscribed doe like verie well of the said mocyon and are willinge to be admitted to the said trade and for better testimony thereof they have hereunto subscribed there names. And it is further agreed that Mr. John Howell Maio' Mr. John Prowse Mr. Richard Dorchester Mr. John Ellacott and Mr. William Martin the younger shall fourthwith answere Mr. Carmarden's letter directed to Sir Thomas Ridgwaie Knight."

"2nd July 1566. At which Courte it is enacted ordeyned established and agreed by the Governo' Consulls and Company before particularie named That none nor any parson or parsons being free of this Societie and Company whatsoever he or they be shall from hensforthe by theymselves or by any their factors, sarvauntes or apprentices lade or ffright any shipp or barke to the parties of Andolosia Byskey Galisia or Portugalle But by hymself onlie or with suche as be free of this Company : Nor that any forryner or stranger nor any other parson or parsons not free of this Company shall lade any parte or porcion of any shipp or barke or be in coplement with any of this Societie and Company to or froo any the parties before mentioned upon payne of every such parson of this Companye so doinge the contrarie to paye and forfeite to this Company for every tyme the somme of Twentie pounds. The one third parte thereof to be to hime that shall present the same and thother two partes to the Company. And if any such faulte before mentioned be founde in any factor sarvaunte or apprentise the forfeite and payne thereof to be levied upon their Maister."

Owners and Masters of Ships not to load with 'wares marchandizes or moneys' belonging to those not free of the Company—To state so in writing on the Charterparties.

"14 March 1576. At this Courte there is certen complayntes made to the Governo' Consulls and Companie by certen Marchauntes of the town of Morles in the parties of Brytaine that diverse inglishe mcnne, covetinge their owne private gayne, doo bye beyonde the seas narrowe lynnen clothe contrarie to the orders in the saide Countrie of Brytaine. Therefore it is nowe at this present Courte enacted and fullie agreed upon by the saide Governo' Consulls and Companye That whatsoever hee bee, free of this Companye (or any others) that after the daye of the kepinge of this present Courte Do bye or bringe over from the parties beyond the Sees unto this realme of Englande, any of the saide narrowe lynnen cloth, That is to say any dowles, grese cloth, or Treger: Shalle paye unto this Companie for everie pece so bought and brought into this realme the some of xs if the same be not of the breadeth of iij quarters of a yarde and a half at the leaste, suche Marchauntes free of this Companye which have heretofore freighted the 'Jonas' and the 'Primerose' of Topsham onelie excepted. And further it is agreed that no person or persons free of this Companye, nor any other whatsoever hee bee shall bye any of the saide narrowe lynnen cloth in any place within this realme to be solde within this Citie of Exon orellswhere upon the like payne of xs for everie pece so bought."

www.ingramcontent.com/pod-product-compliance
Lightning Source LLC
Chambersburg PA
CBHW031737230426
43669CB00007B/377